WHITEOUT

WHITEOUT
recollections on a family of privilege

a memoir by

Hugh Merrill

Spartan Press | Kansas City, MO

Spartan Press
Kansas City, MO 64111
spartanpresskc.com

Spartan
Press

First Edition 11 7 5 3 2 1
ISBN: 978-1-950380-49-7
LCCN: 2019945238
Design, edits and layout: Jeanette Powers
Edits: Rebecca Merrill
stubbornmulepress@gmail.com @stubbornmulepress
Cover & Interior Art: Hugh Merrill

Table of Contents

Power of Privilege

My family grew along a trajectory that defines white privilege and power. A power which has twisted, for the worse, the lives of many. Over generations, my family helped shape the Jim Crow laws in Alabama, convicted the innocent and saved the guilty; they profited from slavery, lynching, racial terror; hired convicts from the prison leasing system and took full advantage of all the other perks that go with wealth and easy access to the powerful.

This is not a story of the past, my cousin John Merrill, is Secretary of State of Alabama is currently running for Senate (2019). He crafted voter ID laws to disenfranchise people of color, immigrants and the poor from their ability to vote. You most likely saw him interviewed on national TV during Alabama's special Senate election (2017), featured on both CNN and FOX. He is a Trump Republican and a Roy Moore supporter. Doug Jones, the moderate and sane Democrat, thankfully won the vacant Senate seat. John Merrill, as Secretary of State, had to go on television and certify the vote.

My great grandfather was an officer in the cavalry of the Confederate States of America under the renowned General Jeb Stewart; he fought at the Battle of Gettysburg, Yellow Tavern and others. He came to Alabama after the Civil War, set up the Pinetucky Goldmine and a law practice in Anniston, Alabama. He saw the power of politics and made it his business to become influential locally. He taught his children to dream bigger.

My grandfather, Hugh D. Merrill, a popular legislator was also an appointed judge, Speaker of the House, and Lieutenant Governor of Alabama. He was the judge in a very famous trial in 1918 that ended with the "legal lynching" of a black solider,

Sergeant Edgar Caldwell. The United States Supreme Court heard the case and let the verdict stand. W.E.B Dubois, one of the founders of the NAACP, was involved. President Woodrow Wilson wrote the Alabama Governor asking for clemency and thousands of others tried to stop this travesty of justice to save the life of Sgt. Caldwell. Their campaign failed.

My grandfather, Big Daddy to me and my siblings, sentenced him to death in a trial that was no more than a sham. The flawed trial provided the cover for due process. The verdict's real intent was to make the long established practice of racial terrorism have the patina, and the vital *precedence*, of legality. "Legal lynching" was a more socially acceptable way to enforce the South's culture of segregation and white supremacy through racial terror. Lynching had moved from the streets and mob to exist as false judicial procedure dished out under the direction of the State.

This process continues today in Alabama and other states. Especially those from the old confederacy, where an easy trail can be charted from slave owner justice, to mob violence and lynching, to sham trials during the Jim Crow era. Inequity continues with the present use of capital punishment, endemic police brutality aimed predominantly against black folks, and more brutal verdicts and sentences against poor defendants.

My uncle, Hugh D. Merrill, Jr., was a long time Alabama state representative and close advisor to Governor George Wallace, famous for standing in the door of the University of Alabama to prevent the enrollment of James Hood, one of the first black students to attempt to break the racial barrier of segregated universities. Uncle Hugh also defended the seven KKK terrorists charged with fire-bombing the Freedom Riders' bus in Anniston, Alabama on Mother's Day in 1961. The defendants and the rest of the mob beat the Freedom Riders with clubs, slashed the tires of the bus and tried to prevent the riders from escaping as the bus burned. A good number of people in the mob were still in their church clothes, having gone straight to the bus terminal from Sunday service. Uncle Hugh represented these men in Federal court where six of them received a suspended sentence to one year probation and an admonishment from the judge to stay away from the Klan. The seventh defendant, Kenneth Adams, also the Grand Wizard of the Alabama KKK, was acquitted.

My father, James W. Merrill, left Alabama for reasons not ever clearly explained. The reasons are vague but carry hints of abusive behavior, perhaps sexual misconduct or sex with some important person's daughter or wife. After World War II, he became a major player in the Agriculture Department in Washington, D.C.. He was in charge of peanuts for the Southeastern United States. He would return to Alabama to have sex with his brother's wife, or wife-to-be, it was never clear; but it did produce my half-brother David. The fact that David was my father's bastard son was bragged about even in front of my mother and I was called "dratsab" as a nick name which, of course, is *bastard* spelled backwards.

As a child, I grew up traveling through the violent, segregated south of the 1950's and 1960's. I saw the southern system of apartheid, visited many small towns with their confederate monuments facing south. I saw the *whites-only* signs on drinking fountains and bathrooms, on hotels and in cafés and stores. I saw the poverty of the share-croppers and drove by chain gangs cleaning ditches and repairing roads. My father and mother were part of the upper crust of the Democratic Party and worked with, and knew by first name, folks like Senator John Sparkman of Alabama, Lyndon B. Johnson, both Robert and John Kennedy, Wernher von Braun the scientist, and Hubert Humphrey. The list goes on and on like a Forrest Gump narrative, only true.

One day I shared with a dear friend a story I'd written about a young indigenous woman and her plight of cultural and sexual violence growing up in the South in the 1950's. My friend replied with a short, curt comment:

This is my story. Write your own story.

At that time my daughter was in law school and had begun a deep dive into our family history; interested to know the details of their lives as legislators and litigators in Alabama. She uncovered the Caldwell case, and the details of Uncle Hugh's involvement in the racist push back to the Civil Rights Movement. The dark episodes continue to trickle in as she does more research. Having uncovered my family's contributions to racial terrorism, to my own privilege, and my blindness to this history I have to recall my own past anew. So now, I keep my eyes open. Now, I tell this story.

This is neither a novel nor a memoir, it is my magical recollection based on the stories I was told and the world I remember. These are my stories, a bit mythical, and based in the culture of my family as experienced by a child, teen and maturing man. This is my story of the power of privilege.

My Birth

I was dead when I finally squirted free from my mother's birth canal. Her thoughts were wild with fear, but not for the loss of the child she had hated for the past 8 months. It had been six years since the birth of her last child, a morose little boy whose eyes haunted her and whose hypersensitivity kept her on constant edge. The silence of the rural clinic was wonderful and appropriate for the birthing of a silent infant. I, the newborn, lay small, blue, wet and bloody on the sheets between my mother's legs.

There were two beds in the clinic, and if the scene were viewed from the location of the ceiling light bulb at the instance of my birth, you would have seen a sweaty and exhausted beauty. A women of 32, propped up by several pillows, spread-eagled on the clinic bed. Her hospital gown had fallen open exposing her firm breasts and white skin. She had a look of pain, yet relief, on her refined face that was framed by wet and matted reddish brown hair. Her covers had fallen to the floor between the bed and the window that looked out on the cow pasture that surrounded the clinic on three sides.

The doctor and her husband, Jim, sat drunk and drinking more Old Crow on the second bed at the instant the blue baby finally made it out and onto the sheets. They leaned forward, spilling the full ashtray that sat between them on the bed, smoke hanging in the thick air. The oversized glass ashtray smashed to the floor of the infirmary, breaking the silence for an instant, but no one seemed shocked by the sound.

Velma, the nurse, stood at the foot of the bed holding a dry towel. Her foot was bouncing, waiting for the doctor to finally hand her the newborn baby, me. There was no movement in the room except for the smoke rising from the stub of a cigarette in Doctor Asher's mouth and the one between the fingers of my father. Their glasses of Old Crow tilted to the spilling point as they leaned forward to look at me.

Doctor Asher's brain suddenly engaged and he moved suddenly, with knowledge and proficiency. He grabbed the dead baby by the feet and yanked me up with such force that my placenta was suddenly pulled down the birth canal right behind me. He held me upside down by the feet with his left hand and reached back with his right hand to grab a half full bottle of Old Crow. He poured the bourbon over me and with several strong whacks to the back and rump I came alive, coughing up yellowish phlegm that splattered over my mother's belly and crotch. She looked at the me in astonished wonder and the anguish of perpetual guilt that would undermine our relationship for decades to come.

Letting Go My "Mothers"

They say you have to be taught to hate, but you also have to be taught to love. Who and how you love is determined by who and how you hate: they cannot be separated. Being raised at the top of Southern society meant that I was cared for by a maid, a black woman, who did all the hard work while my mother tended to *more important* social obligations and concerns. Was I cared for or loved? *Cared for* is most likely the correct phrase. Love is freely given, not purchased, but this small white child did not know the difference. Irene, the maid, knew the reality of Jim Crow life. She knew to keep an emotional distance and she worked to protect herself and her family as best she could from the whims of the master during the slavery era, from Mr. Peckerwood during Jim Crow or the kind and progressive Merrill's in the age just before the New Frontier.

I would play cards by myself on the living room floor. Irene would be watching daytime TV and cleaning the already very clean house, I would not be playing a card game but playing with a deck of cards. Playing with the cards like they were toy soldiers. When I tired of my game, I would leave the cards where they lay, scattered under the coffee table, some laying by the console TV, others half way up the carpeted stairs and many thrown across the living room floor. Like the remnants of a wild game of 52 pickup the cards were strewn in all directions. If I heard Irene coming, I would bolt up and attempt my escape, running toward the front door, hoping she would not notice my mess before I was out the door and gone. But she always did and this scene was played out often.

She would call me back, *Hughboy you get back here an' pick up your toys.* I would fuss, make false promises: *I'll do it when I come back, will you do it,* I'd beg, fuss, say please, stomp my feet, put on my meanest and then saddest face, hunch my shoulders and begrudgingly begin the tiny chore. I felt angry, knew I would be in trouble, not only from Irene, but my parents if I did not obey her. So in total exasperation I stomped about picking up the cards, showing all the fury a 6 year old can at having to do what they do not want. Irene would laugh *Hughboy that sassy way of yours going to get you blow down, you wait and see honey, wait and see, now pick up the cards and then you can go, go as far as your feet can take you.* That calm voice, in southern dialect, soothed my anger and sassy ways. I would hold onto my gruff exterior and keep my mean face glued on tight. She would turn away from cleaning and say *now Hughboy let me see you smile, just a little smile for Irene, just a little laugh. Come on honey you can do it, come on now just pick up the card it only be a minute* and then the routine I knew was coming, showed up.

Come on honey, smile for Irene, I would do all I could not to smile, *come on Hughboy, let me see you laugh, come on now* and I would screw up my face and close my eyes trying not to smile or laugh, *come on honey let me hear a giggle, a little laugh* and then the dam would burst and I would be laughing in torrents, angry at myself for not being able to be angry, losing my pride and distance. I would cave in, cave in to joy. I would find myself a silly wonderful child, laughing like a hyena.

The 'benevolent kindness' of the employers, my parents, was highly erratic and the winds could shift at any moment. There is a vast difference between true friendship, shared love, reciprocal kindness, and mutual respect, and a hired hand. The difference was crystal clear to the *servant*, the nanny, and the maid but only vaguely considered by the white family employing a Negro woman to care for, perhaps even love (or act as though loving) their children. The reality of the relationship was written in stone stronger than the commandments hauled off Mt. Sinai. Irene knew it, better than any of us, and knew it well.

I imagine her telling her husband, *you know what the boy did today, he threw his cards all over the floor, threw a fuss like you never seen, if our children acted like that white folks would not stand for it, he acts just like his father, thinks he owns it all, several good smacks on the anatomy he sits on would take that sassy boy down a peg,* and the story would go on.

The small things that make a mother and child bond were turned over to a servant. Only the child with the bottle in their mouth or crying over a broken toy understood who the real mother was. The child did not know or care to understand the niceties of Southern Society, they only sought love and comfort, and they knew where to find it. For him or should I say me, this was the person you ran to for love, reassurance, to help with the pain of a scraped knee, and who you ran to was The Help. Irene made the lunches for school, was there when I got home and had my snack waiting for me, wanted to hear about my day and was the first to see a drawing, a cutout pumpkin from construction paper, my box of Valentines and all the other elementary school treasures.

When I was younger, prior to going to school, she was busy watching after me. Once I was in school, I got home at 2:00 and she was there to talk and hear about my day. As the grades passed, though, she had less and less to do. Though we lived in a large home in Alexandria, Virginia, it did not need to be dusted, vacuumed and scrubbed every day. Yes, she made the beds, did the wash, watched soaps on TV and snuck toddies from the liquor cabinet, a well-stocked liquor cabinet in the Tiki styled bar in the basement.

Evening discussions by my parents addressed the new *problem of Irene*, there was not enough for her to do and my mother was set on letting her go. As I listened, the idea of letting Irene go, so central a person in my life, seemed frightening. *Let her go.* I was not sure what that meant, but I knew it was not good. They had *let go* of numerous dogs, but they had all had the bad habit of crapping on the rug, digging up the roses and azalea bushes or some other capital offence. They had to be let go, that's one thing for the dogs but not Irene. She was not called *mom* or *mother,* but played that part well. My mother was a distant and vague presence in my young life but Irene was the *mother*, the one who scolded and enforced, the nurse, the maker of lunches and snacks, the one who held me and the one who showed care, showed concern and pride in my small accomplishments. Irene, *Irene*, it was not just a name it was more *motherish*. Irene was married to a porter at the railroad station, had kids of her own. Who took care of them? I never thought about that till decades later. Irene, graceful Irene, ageless Irene, she was an adult to me. I had little idea of the complexity and meanings in age. People over the age of 18 were smart adults, grownups, and a mystery to a 6-year-old.

Irene was beautiful, you can see it in the single old photo I remember. The Merrill's had photos of family that went back to the Confederate Army. They had the money to purchase photographs, tintypes in small cases from itinerate photographers. When it was possible, they bought cameras and took family photos, and my father bought the first commercial Polaroid Camera. But Irene, the woman who raised me, cared for me, was in only one, she stood smiling at the camera with one arm outstretched on the fireplace mantle, her white blouse open showing the beautiful cleavage of perhaps a 30 year-old. Her arms were strong muscled, unlike the sausage arms of white women who picked up nothing heavier than the yellow pages.

Her skirt was slightly twisted and she wore no shoes, she smiled, not in embarrassment or shyness, for I cannot imagine Irene as being shy, she smiled with resignation, knowledge and understanding. She must have been told by my father to smile for only he would have taken the photo. She smiled like someone hearing the prompt *say cheese* and that uncomfortable frozen smile performed across her uncomfortable but compliant face.

The evening conversations on Irene's fate became more and more pronounced. My mother demanded to let her go and my father resisted. The complaint my mother flung was that the maid did nothing but sit all day and watch soaps and drink our whiskey. That she did not clean or do the laundry correctly, the beds were not made as they should be, her work was not up to our standards. My truth hung in the air above my head alone in the understanding of the child that needed her and expected her to always be there.

Their truth was likely something else. Sex, of course, was the root of many problems in my family. I somehow knew about sex and it is attached darkly to my earliest memories. So, my father was screwing Irene, driving home from the Agriculture Department while my mother worked as a receptionist and typist for Senator John Sparkman from Alabama, a long time Merrill friend of the family. My mother was no saint either. She was beautiful in her 30's with an amazing figure, at least while dressed in a girdle and pointy bra. She was John Sparkman's lover. You have seen John Sparkman and most likely never knew it, if you have seen Jack Kennedy riding in the open air car from the inauguration down Pennsylvania Avenue on that freezing cold day, the man in the top hat next to Kennedy is John Sparkman, my mother's lover.

I came home from school and my parents were there which was very odd and took me aside and told me that Irene would not be coming back. They said I was old enough to take care of myself after school, that if I needed anything the neighbors, the Stevens, Olkes, the Beers and the Heffners were there to help. They told me we would have a new maid. It was then that I realized the true worth of Irene. She was a maid not a mother, a disposable addition to the family, no more than a disobedient family dog that had to be let go or put down.

We would have a new maid, Iza, coming to clean house and that from this day forward I would have to make my own bed. Making a bed became a lesson for joining the Army, I was instructed by my father, a lieutenant that had trained Black troops in Virginia during WWII, how important it was to make a bed correctly. To make the covers fit so tight that a dime, when flipped on the surface, would bounce up like it had fallen on a hard wood floor. I never did get it even close to correct and was sure I should never join the army.

So Iza came to the house and was not at all like beautiful Irene, she was short, round, and large breasted. She did not dress in starched white shirts and a black skirt, but flower print dresses that tented her rounded and sagging figure. While she never could replace my first Irene, she quickly became my source for comfort. Held on her lap, I laughed and was fearless. We joked and talked and she was kind and loving. Not Irene, but always wonderful and there for me.

I swung the bat and hit our neighbor Richard directly under his eye. He ran up behind me and into the backward arc of my swinging at an imaginary pitch from an imaginary pitcher. I would learn 10 years later, in the ring, that it was a boxer's cut. The bat had barely grazed the bone just under the eye opening up a cut like a knife, a cut that so many Irish boxers endure with their sharp cheekbones. As a 8 or 9 year old it scared the hell out of me and poor Richard sat on the ground in a pool of blood. Blood was everywhere, his shirt was instantly soaked. I do not know how he got up the stairs to his house for I ran toward my house to hide in the arms of Iza, ashamed of what I had done, frightened I would go to hell and be whipped for hitting Richard with a baseball bat, frightened of the unknown a feeling that would follow me through life. I simply wanted to disappear, not exist, simply not be.

Iza rescued me and gave me strength to do the right thing, she hugged me and I cried into her shoulder as I sat on her lap, she stroked the back of my head and talked to me, telling me it would be all right which I did not entirely believe but at least was quieted and stopped balling. She helped me blow my nose, calm down and talked to me, soothing my fears and showing as best she could that it might not have been my fault. She was not sure what had occurred. Mrs. Brown called to let us know that Richard was being stitched up by Doctor Bowman who had driven over from his office near the Center Movie Theatre. It took three stitches to close the wound, and a bowl of ice cream and a cookie to calm Richard down. Iza walked me back to the stairs of Richard's house holding my hand and telling me to be a man and go tell Richard I was sorry and check on how he was.

I climbed the stairs to the front door just a little less frightened than when I had grazed him with the bat and saw the river of blood. I looked back at Iza for support and rang the doorbell, Richard's mother opened the door, did not invite Iza in but smiled in her direction and hugged me. She took me into the house, Richard sat in front of his ice cream and smiled. He and I were ok, had survived a moment in the ever-changing path toward growing old. I sat next to him and we were soon laughing and enjoying ice cream and cookies. When I headed home, Iza was back at the house waiting for me, standing on the front porch. My deep affection for her now that things were ok had turned to childish indifference and I ran past her into the living room in search of some new adventure.

I can look back from the vantage point of a life almost lived and imagine her face, her shaking her head slowly thinking with fear and knowledge what would have happened if it had been her son Eldridge, a black kid. What would have happened if he had swung the bat and hit Richard. Or if Eldridge had been cut how they would have laid him on their kitchen table and closed the bleeding with pressure and tape, no doctor Bowman would have visited. Anyway, the next day Richard and I were taken to the Barnum and Bailey Circus, back then still performed under wax coated canvas tents put up with the help of elephants. Now that I look back I think the tickets and circus must have been planned weeks ahead but then as a 7 or 8 year old I thought it was because of the swing of a bat hitting the bull's eye that we got to go.

A couple of years later, at the age of 11, I came home and Iza was gone, like Irene but without an explanation. I was learning the deeper lesson of my society: black folks are expendable. But the lesson went deeper still: that all people, family, friends and hired hands were expendable and to be kept at a safe emotional distance. Don't invest deeply in love for it does not last.

We moved to a new home across town, after my father's major lung operation he could no longer make it up the steps from the street to the house. So, we moved to Fountain Street and hired a new maid to come in one day a week. A beautiful, young, 18-year-old black woman. I did not even get to know her name, though my father came home for lunch on Thursdays when she worked.

Elephant

Being drunk in the 1950's was funny, every house in our neighborhood had a finished basement with a bar in it. The parents would often have cocktail parties and it was odd to see the Captains, Colonels and the other men we addressed as *sir* in Bermuda shorts, argyle socks and deck shoes. The basement cocktail bars often had paintings of dogs playing poker, a delight for the kids and a disgrace for the wives, though I think in reality everyone loved the poker playing dogs. These were not casual people, they were formal, and had just survived WWII. But they did know how to drink and have a hair of the dog that bit you the morning after. Drinking was fun and funny.

It was the pink elephant that was king of drinking and getting drunk, dancing pink elephants on party trays flying without wings through a pattern of cocktails, fruit and liqueur bottles. There were pink elephants everywhere on coasters, trays, cocktail dresses, cocktail shakers and anything associated with drinking including the names of many bars, the Pink Elephant Lounge was a popular name. The cocktail napkins often had cute pink elephant jokes like: how do you catch a pink elephant? Hide behind the bar and make noise like you're making a martini, you will catch one. It was the age of the lamp shade hat for drunks and pink elephants.

My mother and father were deeper into drinking than most, both alcoholics. So, we lived on an emotional rollercoaster fueled by our parents, out of control and angry. Angry at the stupid stuff of life, like had you paired your socks and put them in your sock drawer correctly. Everything had its set of rules and they seemed to change depending on the amount of booze consumed, time of day and degree of general anger and bitterness they harbored to each other or the world.

Our emotional rollercoaster became steeper and more frightening when we took our summer vacations driving south with my older sister and brother in the back seat of the Packard Clipper. On the floor behind the driver's seat, my father's seat, was a tin Coke-a-Cola cooler holding ice, whiskey and goodies. I sat between my parents, my father driving, my mother in the passenger seat. Me in the middle on a raised arm rest like a projectile ready to be shot through the windshield. Of course, there were no seat belts then and if there were we would not have worn them, it would not have been our way.

Our house was large and everyone had their own room, plus the basement and backyard There was a near-by woods the family valued to keep distance from the neighbors. In the car, we were on top of each other and the slightest miscalculation, inadvertent use of the window, opening the cooler and looking in, spilling a drink or, well, anything, led to my father swinging, hitting, yelling and general disaster.

The long days of driving on two lane country roads was torture. This was prior to the national highway system, we drove along old route 1/301 running from Maine to Florida. Route 95, the super four lane highway was still being built. So, we crawled along at 45 if we were lucky, had to go through every small town along the way and get stuck behind vehicles and tractors. Passing while stuck in a line of other cars was perhaps as dangerous as anything a person could do in a lifetime. Drinking, anger, southern heat and humidity, no air conditioning, would lead to an angry and frustrated stomp on the gas, my father swerving into the lane of opposite traffic, passing four cars and a tractor and nearly missing a head-on collision. This occurred time and again as we puttered south from Washington DC to Florida and on to Alabama.

We drove and endured the hours of playing cow poker, reading Burma Shave signs. My father, in his happier drunk moments, would slam on the brakes of the car on some rural country road in south Alabama, jump out and point into a field of peanuts or soybeans and scream something about seeing pink elephants. Then he would force everyone, except my mother, out of the car and we would run in the sun and heat, up and down the road a bit, do a Chinese Fire Drill running around the car then as quickly as we could jump back into our seats, zooming off. Such shenanigans most likely saved us from going crazy and killing each other.

The Burma Shave signs were a treat, they lined up multiple signs on the curve of a rural road the first sign would read *Jar so big*, next, *the cost so small*, then next, *coolest*, then *smoothest*, lastly *shave of all*, finally *Burma Shave*. It was fun to read these Burma Shave jingles but the real thrill were the larger road signs for See Rock City painted on barn roofs, or South of the Border bill boards. South of the Border so named because it was just south of the North Carolina border. It was more than a motel, it was a true home-grown attraction. The signs started 500 miles out in Virginia, themed in a faux Mexican style. Pedro was the caricature of a Mexican bandido, inviting you to stop at this mini golf, motel museum, amusement park, truck stop, gas station, fireworks store and more. As the long slow miles in the heat of the car slid by the closer we got to this attraction we marveled at the signs designating the distance with silly puns like:

You never sausage a place
you're a wiener
at South of the Border.

We would always stop but it was mid-day so we never spent the night and after an hour or so headed back to the car and drove further south, soon passing a billboard just a bit further down the road, put up by the KKK, welcoming you to South Carolina.

This gimmick to get Yankees to stop and spend some cash on foolishness, choose this gas station over the next, led to some amazing inventions and advertisements. The world's worst golf course which was no more than a driving range in a field of cows. The best was *See Red Bat* only 25 cents, for miles this Gulf station had signs with a graphic of a huge red bat flying about, *don't miss it* only 50 miles to the world's largest red bat, 10 miles *see the red bat, see red bat 5 miles*, 500 feet *STOP SEE RED BAT*. We pulled in, piled out of the car and were running over each other to pay our 25 cents, our quarters to see the bat, up a wooden ramp we crept and saw a 55-gallon wooden barrel with a metal screened cage to keep the bat in and you out. Walking cautiously up the ramp with signs on the hand rails warning not to put your hands or fingers in the cage. Paintings of the gigantic bat framed the platform with its drum and bat cage. We walked up and there was a filling station attendant standing next to the cage, we gave him our quarters and leaned forward to look and he screamed and scared the shit out of us. Everyone laughed and we tried again. Finally, the moment came when we looked over the edge of the 55-gallon drum and through the wire screen and saw a painted red *baseball* bat. That was all there was to it, but it was hysterical, one of the great moments on a family trip designed in hell for the most part. This was the rural south of the 1950's.

Back in the car after buying and drinking Cokes, RC Cola or Dr. Pepper sodas bought from a vending station filled with blocks of ice and cold water. The bottles hung on a metal rack from their necks which kept the soda wonderfully cold. Then it was time to move on and we drove south. Some place in rural Alabama or perhaps Georgia, in a world of pine forests. The trees were owned by Wear Houser paper company, trees to be cut down for America's insane hunger and need for cheap paper. We sped along. In places the trees grew like stalks of corn in straight rows and literally popped by the car, in other places the trees grew in a more natural, less industrial manner.

Some place along this stretch in the middle of nowhere with few, if any other cars passing, my father did his drunken Chinese Fire Drill and pink elephant routine. Except this time, he seemed to have really lost his mental facilities, he did not just get out of the car as usual but climbed through a rusted barbwire fence and ran off into the Georgia woods. Even my debutant mother got out and looked worriedly into the pines, surely thinking that her drunk husband had lost it. Soon enough as we stood by the side of the road looking toward the woods, seeing only dragon flies and red wing black birds dart in and out of the high grass beyond the wire fence, my father suddenly reappeared. He was running with torn pants, grinning from ear to ear like the crazy man he was, out of control. He grabbed me and lifted me over the fence and waved for the rest to follow and headed back into the woods, dragging me by one hand.

My brother and sister followed, picking their way through the barbed wire and tracing our path into the dark pines. We did not have to go far to see what had caused the commotion. There in a clearing, the earth covered with brown pine needles shaded completely by the tall pines on all sides, stood three elephants. Not only were they elephants, but they were totally decked out in pink, purple and silver spangles, and had tiaras on their massive heads. We stood in the Georgia woods looking at circus elephants, no roustabouts in sight, no circus in sight, just three decked out cool looking elephants. We, of course, walked up and touched them, petted their course hairy legs and shoulders. They were eating, chewing like a cow chews its cud. They paid us no attention. We stood looking up into their moist eyes, cautiously touched them, were silent and awe struck. Out of the forest came the circus crew to get their wayward elephants back. They had simply pulled up their stakes and walked off and no one had at first noticed. We watched the men take the elephants by their trunks using some form of a hooked stick and simply walk the elephants back toward their circus camp on the other side of the woods.

We headed back to the car excited, told and retold the story for years and even now. Looking back from today I cannot imagine what my father thought when he actually glimpsed pink elephants in the Georgia woods, when he slammed on the brakes, backed up the car and ran into the forest. Had he not found them, after having seen them, would he have questioned his own sanity, would he have quit drinking and found God? Who knows? But he found them, they were real and not the imaginary pink elephant hallucination of napkin art. His trajectory in life went unchanged and we kept heading to Alabama.

On Becoming Presbyterian

God and Jesus did not make much of an appearance in our home. There certainly was no Bible study or even references to God, Jesus or the Bible in our everyday life. God entered the home through two prayers. One was at the weekly family dinner, or better understood as Sunday Dinner. It was the only time the family sat down together, and a dangerous and stressful time it was. The second prayer happened when my mother put me to bed. Of course there was Church, but church was more of a social occasion, though we children knew the basic bible stories. We celebrated Christmas as more a greedy festival of hot toddies, eggnog and whiskey, crème de menthe on ice cream with an over decorated tree under which were crammed layer on layer of brightly wrapped presents. The real deity of our house was drinking and looking good.

Whiskey, whiskey, you killed my dear old dad if you don't kill me you'll surly wish you had. When I get drunk just lay me in my bunk cause it's nobody's business but my own.

This WWII camp song was on occasions my bed time story and lullaby rolled into one. As I recall, Dad did not put me to bed often, that was my mothers' chore. But when he did, he came in with whiskey in hand and ready to sing. He had a pretty good voice, so my mother said, but I was too young to notice. He would sing more to himself than to me anyway. He was loud, sat in a chair, not on the bed, and rang out first with the ditty: *Mares eat oats, does eat oats and little lambs eat ivy, fiddlie fiddie, too, wouldn't you.*

Then came some song about little fishes swimming over a dam and I think he pronounced it *d-a-m-n*. It made him laugh, though I did not get the joke. Then came the last song. Three songs is all you got, it was a three song performance, seemingly being sung to some invisible audience in a bar surrounding a piano, a dream from his memory. The finale was his beloved

Camp Certainly song, from when he was with *his* Negro Troops at a training base in Hopewell, Virginia.

Whiskey, whiskey, you killed my dear old dad if you don't kill me you'll surly wish you had. When I get drunk just lay me in my bunk cause it's nobody's business but my own. When I am sober just do the same thing over, cause it's nobody's business but my own.

He would sing to the walls and then abruptly leave, lights out, no prayer, no mention of God, no praying for relatives, just a command of *go to sleep* and out he went, door closing behind him, leaving me in a partly darkened room with my covered wagon night light. The light that one day caught on fire and burned itself to a char.

My mother, though distant, was more attentive to me and my religious education. We prayed together saying this famous little prayer outloud:

Now I lay me down to sleep,
I pray the Lord my soul to keep,
If I die before I wake,
I pray the Lord my soul to take.

Now I lay me down to sleep, which as a child in a southern world I took as one word nowalaymi or not even a word but more of a chant. A chant that seemed to have not meaning or relation to the next line. The prayer was frightening for I thought it concerned my imminent death or forecast it to come some night, perhaps this week or next but a certainty or why would it be in a prayer if it were not true? It had to be true.

Nowalaymi
Down to sleep
I pray the Lord my soul to keep,
If I die before I wake,
I pray the Lord my soul to take.

Then came a series of God bless Grandfather, Grandmother, Big Daddy and so on then lights out, the door closed and I lay their waiting to die.

Someone had made sure that I understood as a child I would go to heaven but once I became older I would have to be judged. As a kid who flunked the first grade and started fights, stole stuff, broke off roses from other people's bushes and broke some windows, after God's judgment, was for sure going to hell. I considered suicide even at seven but I figured I had till I was ten. I figured when you hit double digits you were then no longer a kid and so that's when God's judgment got you. So, I still had some time. But perhaps like the prayer suggested, I would die in my sleep as a mere child.

The only other prayer was said at dinner on Sunday and it, too, was a curve ball that was off the plate and in the dirt. My father, being the head of the *family*, would say this prayer at Sunday Dinner which was held each week around 2:00 in the afternoon. Often served was fried chicken and mashed potatoes, green beans, back eyed peas and, of course, gravy.

Lord make us thankful for these and all our blessings for Christsakes, amen and of course the Christsakes was intoned as if an exasperated, pissed off sailor had just dropped his gold bars overboard by mistake.

Coming from Alabama we were Baptists but that morality, responsibility and faith were not ingrained or much thought about. Desire, greed, anger and power were our real values. Getting one over on the other guy at work or at the country club seemed to have value. From my youngest time, I remember not funny stories, not big fish stories, but how *I did this to them* stories. My Father and my sister would tell lavish stories of hurting or undoing another person of putting them down in public and coming out the momentary winner. Humility was not a family trait.

Outside of the family and social circle, our contacts where love and respect were at a minimum, existed the deserving poor and for this group, who we did not have any real or deep connection with, my father seemed to have authentic care. He helped write legislation and produce programs to help small farmers and sharecroppers. These hard-working men, women and children he had seen growing up and he wanted to better their lives.

My parents had seen real poverty and discrimination. They saw the thousand-mile stare in the hungry eyes of jobless women and men in the train yards, they saw on the edge of every town bum camps, fires burning, cooking a hobo stew of thin broth and taters or beans, never bacon but perhaps some fatback. They saw sharecroppers unable to feed their families. They also saw the success and meaning of FDR's social programs built to elevate common folks from this desperate poverty. But they saw all this from a safe distance. They were untouched by the depression and cruised through WWII. It was one big party for my Dad, from recruiting women for Women's Army Corp, to strangely ending up training black troops, about as far as you could fall in the military during my father's time without being put before a firing squad and shot for treason. No doubt about it, he screwed some General's wife or daughter and got caught. Perhaps I have another half-sibling out there. Because he was the son of privilege, his father being the Lieutenant Governor of Alabama, he had more than a soft cushion for when he fell and he fell and bounced back to prosperity many times.

When my family ended up in Washington DC, or rather Alexandria, Virginia to be correct, they were near the upper crust of political social circles. They were members of the Belle Haven Country Club and the Baptist Church. They were moderate Southerners which meant they knew change had to come, but had a very go-slow attitude regarding that change. They did seem to despise the ranker forms of white supremacy and KKK styled racial terror. They loved To Kill a Mockingbird and Atticus Finch's portrayal of southern courage and values. They saw themselves through that lens. But we, of course, made the trip to Stone Mountain Georgia while traveling through Atlanta to see the warped romantic portrayal of Southern Heritage with its huge carving of Lee, Jackson Jefferson Davis and Jeb Stewart, the unfinished carving on the face of the huge rock boulder inspired something in my father. I thought it looked lame compared to Mount Rushmore, which I had only scene in photographs. My father was a man caught between two worlds: the old South and the Kennedy New Frontier. Wanting things to remain, yet wanting to be part of the change and benevolently help poor people and Negros.

The word *Nigger* or even *Negra* was never part of his vocabulary. Having trained Negro troops, some who died in battle in Italy, perhaps contributed to his deep personal respect, even love for "them" but they certainly could not be invited to live next door, or attend our schools. They remained "them": the other, separate and not truly equal in his mind. He understood their lives were tough and the work that they often did was the lowest and hardest with the least respect attached to it. They did not need to have their lives made tougher by further blatant cruelty, terror and disrespect. *But let's not go too fast, give folks time to change, to grow into change*, he more than once pronounced.

So, like all political families in the South, you went to church on Sunday and on Monday you did what was necessary. In my family history, that would include condemning an innocent black man to be hanged, hiring workers from the convict leasing system and crafting Jim Crow laws. There seemed no ethical or moral question to consider when it came to race, no contradictions in forced separation and limited opportunity for "them" in all areas for life. Church was a social obligation for my father's family and so it was with our family. Each Sunday we would dress in ties and sports jackets, and shiny shoes. My parents, my older brother and sister and I would go to the Baptist Church in Alexandria, Virginia, it was the era of the civil rights movement: 1957.

The Baptist church was a new building, a large brick rectangle with a spire and cross on top. A large structure easily holding more than 500 worshipers. My mother was a debutant from Tampa, Florida and lived in a world of mannerisms and correct social behavior. She knew how to eat with the correct utensil, the salad folk was for salads. Never said a mean word, but was, I am sure, I know, filled with fears and her own dangerous devils. Including living and picking up after my father. The worst thing for her was to be embarrassed or judged by others for rude, nasty, frightful behavior and this Sunday she would have all those voices and fears come tumbling down on her. Of what friends my alcoholic parents had, many would be lost this Sunday morning at the 11:00 service.

It was a bright day in May, beautiful with the dogwoods in bloom. It was Pentecost Sunday, the Sunday for speaking in tongues. The honeysuckle in the woods near my home perfumed the air but the air this Sunday in the Baptist church stunk of racist ignorance and hate. The hate was about to pour down in buckets from the pulpit.

I was seven, understood some things, but misunderstood most. We sat in the same order as when we went to the movie theatre: my father on the aisle, me next, my mother, then my sister and my brother, a brooding and absent young man, off in his own imaginary world. The church, like each Sunday, was crowded and after the usual singing, giving, praying and singing the minister started his sermon. This Sunday it was based in the books of Acts, concerning Pentecost. Reverend Brian W. Jones Jr. was a youngish looking man with a pointed, bird of prey face and snide grin for a smile. He stood high in the pulpit, self-important beyond pride's limits.

Pentecost is God's gift to you. The holy spirit was given to each of us, all across the world, on that long-ago day in Jerusalem. God came down...

I drifted off, taking the prayer book out of the rack on the back of the pew and opened it. I was not interested in reading but only looking at the pattern of the words and paragraphs. I enjoyed the black and white patterns of rivers and lakes as typographers referred to the pathways in blocks of type. I had invented a game of chase in school, instead of reading, which was significantly difficult for me, I played *chase*. With my finger I would trace out the white roads diagonally between the lines of sentences, finding escape routes, passages between the words and sentences. Pretending I was being chased, driving a car through the paragraphs of prayer. I was always escaping from some undefined monsters. Absorbed completely in my imaginary game in school, I was always embarrassed when the teacher called on me to read, for I was lost deeply in my own interior world.

Words rang out over my head, some I followed, other times I drifted back into my game. Then I heard Rev. Jones painting an amazing picture of drunken church people dancing about and speaking in tongues, in unknown and foreign languages. Seemingly drunken people screaming and babbling with flames of fire coming out of there head. This great image enraptured me and so the flaming insane ancient Christians became the monsters chasing my pretend car through the text of prayers.

The spirit was on and in them and 3000 came forward that day to be Baptized, he bellowed, and the church folk nodded and gasped *mmm 3000, praise Jesus.*

I raced my imaginary car between sacred words being chased by imaginary flaming Christian monsters. As long as I was quiet, I would not get in trouble. It did not matter that I did not listen or learn, what mattered was to only be good and quiet. Success was to be a good, well-mannered boy.

They who spoke in tongues became disciples,
leaving their lands to travel the world,
speaking new languages and converting others
all over the world
bringing the holy spirit to all of mankind.

There was then an unnatural long pause and I looked up from my game at the silent church and, breaking the tension, Rev. Jones thundered on:

But let us consider the mark of Cain, for not all peoples are the same
God has different plans for different types of peoples
different races and colors of peoples.

Soon the meaning became clear to the congregation, 1957, was a year of Massive Resistance to civil rights in the South. On the floor of the United States Senate, Senator Strom Thurman of South Carolina had just completed the longest single filibuster in history. 24 hours and 18 minutes he had stood and read and talked to try and prevent the passage of the voting rights act of 1957, an act of Congress that called for greater equality in voting rights for Negros and the poor. The attempts to integrate southern schools, of allowing Negros to vote was not new to me, it was on the TV and radio news every night. What was said was of little interest to me, but the images from Little Rock of soldiers in the streets, white mobs chasing and attacking a small group of Negro children was riveting, frightening and beyond understanding. Words, important words, floated out of the TV, the radio, and I heard them in daily conversation and now here in the confines of the Baptist Church: civil rights, segregation, equality, integration, heritage and more were taking on a distinctive meaning.

Those with the mark of Cain, the mark of dark skin, are not worthy of our schools! Do not have the aptitude or knowledge to vote, their votes can be bought for a drink of whiskey! They are not part of our community with the right to decide civic and national political issues. They are more child-like and like children they need discipline and guidance. Only brother Strom Thurman stood up to filibuster this so-called voting rights bill and...

And my father stood up and in a loud powerful voice, said *Enough of this nonsense, I have never heard such foolishness from the pulpit and let me be clear on this...* My mother sat with head down, embarrassed to the very core of her being. I looked up at him and imagined flames of fire coming from his head but he was not like the first Christians speaking in tongues, this Pentecost it was English with a southern laced drawl. Father continued, *with God as my witness, let me say I will never set foot in this Baptist Church again or any Baptist church.*

He grabbed my hand and pulled me up, my sister and brother were cowering while trying to stand. I watched my mother in tears, with fear in her gestures, rise to her feet confused and try in vain to disappear, to make this all stop, go away. We stepped out from our seats, in the pew, into the aisle of the church in dead silence, stood before every one's criticizing eyes, looking aghast at the Merrill's and the silly grins on the faces of their children. My mother was shamed to death while my father, beaming and proud, marched us out of the sanctuary. We walked down the steps of the church, across the grass to the parking lot and climbed into our large pink Packard and headed home. The next Sunday we were members of the Presbyterian Church.

The Monday after our great schism, after the end of being Baptist, after a Sunday evening of my father's drunken bragging and belligerence, my life returned to its normal routine. When I returned from school at 2:00 Irene was there to care for me. For four years, since I was a toddler, she had been there. I knew her touch, her kiss on my forehead, her hug, and compassion, better than my mother's attempts and far better than my father. This black woman provided love without critique: no scolding, love without a demand for good behavior or being told to sit still or be quiet or to hush. Her skin was dark, beautiful, but the racists' views were already strong, even in this young boy. Racism was not words, not a vocabulary of terms and explanations, it was daily life: Negros cannot go to my church, dip their bodies in *our* swimming pools, sit and eat at *our* restaurants, or go to George Mason Elementary School. The restrictions of space, place, time, even simply salutations, supported systems for separation and hierarchy. I loved Irene, but already accepted her innate separation and lesser-ness as part of life.

My greatest disappointment on becoming a Presbyterian was the baptism. It seemed I now needed to be baptized quickly, so the first week after joining the new church I was scheduled for the ritual, one that I did not really understand or care for. Just several drops of water on my head while I sat on my mother's lap in the darkened office of some reverend. I had hoped to be dunked in the pool at the Baptist church. I loved water, loved the Gulf of Mexico and the pool at every motel we stayed at on our summer trips south, loved to swim and bathe, not shower. Drops of water on the forehead was lame.

My first Sunday in Sunday school, a required part of becoming a member of the church, went badly for my mother but was a victory for me, when I did not know I was even playing a game. My mother and father sat in on this first Sunday school class and watched as we learned some simple Christian story, perhaps about Noah or Moses, seems to me we were given pages from a coloring book and crayons. It was not fun but it was ok. At some point the teacher asked if anyone would like to sing a song, this must have been a weekly practice to teach the children the lyrics of hymns song in the big church. One girl with curly brown hair and a child's choir voice sang Jesus Loves Me This I Know, and the rest of the children joined in. The teacher asked the question again, *would anyone like to sing a song* and my hand shot up. As the new kid with a smile, he called on me. I stood tall like my father at the Baptist church, imagining fire flaming from my head and sang for all I was worth:

Whiskey, Whiskey, you killed my dear old dad if you don't kill me you'll surely wish you had, when I get drunk just lay me in my bunk cause it's nobody's business but my own.

My mother stood horror-stricken as she had in the Baptist Church. My father was roaring in laughter and the rest of the children were near tears. The teacher, she stood in the middle of the room repeating: *no, no no no, please no.* How we exited the class room I do not remember. I was for once praised by my father. This became the childhood moment that defined me a person in his eyes. For a moment I was his pal, not just his offspring. From that Sunday on, I never had to return to Sunday School. I sat in the balcony alone, looking down on the congregation and playing the chase and escape game with the lakes and rivers of the Bible, hymnal and prayer book.

My Mother, my Aunt, the Twins?

By the time I was 9 we had moved from the hilltop house on Argyle Drive and the two women (maids), Irene and Iza who had taken care of me were in the past but never to be forgotten. I had learned quickly and deeply that trust is the foundation of intimacy and love and that you should beware and trust no one. Instead of trust, I joined in the masquerade party built on a life of lies by putting on a man's face, not crying, and learning to be impervious to hurt and feelings. Dishonesty and indifference are a better path to survival. Yet beneath my happy child's mask, was estrangement and injury, with more of the failure of love's promise to come.

I have seen children put to bed at night by their mothers and, like the Virgin Mary putting Jesus in the straw, it was done with care, love and grace, with humor and patience. I had seen images on the silver screen, from movies in the 1950's. I saw soldiers dying on the field of battle taking a drag from their last smoke and then crying *mom* and dying theatrically. Motherly love, the symbol of peace, sentimental joy and safety was an ideal for me, not a daily experience.

Let me say from the start my mother did not have a sister and certainly not a twin sister. In fact, we did have some family, grandparents, aunts and cousins on my father's side but we were distant and not an extended, caring community. Our family was a perfect documentation of the privatized patriarchal nuclear unit. For a child there were neither family nor friends of my parents you could turn to for help and understanding. There was only us, stuck on an island of abuse and violence, loving each other as we had been instructed too.

Her joke was not funny. My mother was a bit different than the saintly mothers waiting for their boys to return from the battles of WWII. My mother's thoughtless joke was weird and unjust; I think she thought her joke was funny and not disturbing to the frightened child bravely cowering beneath the sheets. I was a scared child, though others from the outside thought I was brave, quick to anger and quick to throw a punch, brave in sports and in the ring but all of these actions were part of a deeper loss of self and a fear of the world. Even the places that should have been areas of refuge frightened me, my house frightened me at night or in the day, only the living room seemed safe with the TV droning cartoons. All the rest was a mystery of danger and fear. If I had to go get something for my parents, even in the adjoining room, it was, for me, an act of immense bravery to go into the dark dining room and get a newspaper or hat or take a dish off the table and bring it into the kitchen.

The TV played hours of World War II footage, stories, and documentaries from Victory at Sea to the 20th Century with Walter Cronkite's reassuring voice. This boy was not one of these heroes, I was a fool's fool, and going to bed in my dark room was a provoking experience. My mind was filled with unspecified fears, formless, fears I could only understand as ghostly memories that could not be fully identify and could not quite be put in focus.

These fears were compounded by my mother's bedroom routine. I had to do all the normal stuff bath, brush, dress and such on my own. The bathroom which was the best-lit and brightest room in the house, was a safe zone where I could see all, there were no dark corners, the tub filled with water and toys. Here, I was safe.

Once in bed, my mother would come in and tell me *good night*. It was a short and disconcerting experience, when I was younger she used to help me say my prayers, that *now I lay me down to sleep* prayer. The scary one that mentions dying at night, *if I die before I wake*, that line hovered in my spirit and mind erasing all the other words and images. The rest was said by memory, mechanically, but the die before you wake line was crystal clear in its possibility. Now at nine or ten, I was too old to pray that child's prayer. It had drifted into the past and I was expected to make my own connection with God each night.

God, the vague and unwanted presence soaring about in heaven, sending most people to damnation in hell's fires. I felt I would be next, for I was failing at school and was a kind of bad kid. I was known for turning on people's garden hoses and letting them run, breaking school windows with well-thrown rocks and digging up other people's gardens for the hell of it. When caught, as always happened, I was pronounced a coward and stupid. But one goes on with life playing the cards they are thrown. God did not seem to me to have a great deal of patience with children like myself. So I would climb into the lower bunk of my bunk bed, get under the covers, the light from the hall flowing through the open door keeping the bedroom in a soft half-light, and wait for my Mother to come tell me good night.

It was now that the fun began for her, she would tell me that she loved me and to sleep tight and then casually, as she left the room, she would say *by the way I am not your mother tonight but her twin sister*. I would laugh, which she must have taken as good fun, thinking we were playing a game and that no harm was done. I would protest *no, you're my mother*. She would insist that she was my mom's sister. This exchange, banter, would go on for four or five minutes. She would be leaning on the door jam, all at once say *ok, have it your way, I am your mom*. Then with a flip of her hair and a little annoyed, as if I had failed her in not believing that she was my Mom's twin, would leave the doorway of my room heading either downstairs or back to her room. Leaving me, leaving me in doubt.

On Training Black Troops, WWII

With his wife, kids and family left behind him, and that has a variety of meanings, my Father graduated from office candidate school as a Lieutenant and his first posting was Atlanta, Georgia. His father, Big Daddy to me and the rest of the family, was a former state judge and a Lieutenant himself. He was Lieutenant Governor of Alabama, a state legislator, lawyer and principal owner of Pinetucky Mine, as well as a number of other interests. He was a man trusted to do the right thing, not the moral thing, but the politically right thing, the correct thing to keep the power structure safe and white rich folks in power.

The Merrill family had a deep history with privilege and power in a time that it could be easily wielded. So, it was wheedled to get my father into Officer Candidate School in the Army and then to make sure he did not have to serve as a foot solider in Europe or in the war with Japan: he had a more important job than killing Nazis or the Japanese, he was put in charge of recruiting women for the WAC, the Women's Army Corp, in the southeastern district. He was handsome, athletic, cultured in that Irish southern manner, well-connected and well to-do. He had a car and a driver to drive him across the states of Georgia and Alabama so he could meet with groups of women and 18 year old girls and articulate the importance of what their contribution to the war should be. Which often meant their contribution would begin by crawling into the back seat of his car or his hotel bed to raise the morale of the aforementioned Lieutenant James W. Merrill.

For every solider in the field, in the line of fire, it took seven, or was it ten, support personnel to keep them there. Nurses were almost always women, as were typists and stenographers, bean counters and paper shufflers, secretaries and receptionists.

Most black troops were cooks, porters, truck drivers and both were subject to systemic mistreatment. So, women, like Negro soldiers, were excluded from many opportunities, used and abused, and yet both were amazingly patriotic.

The war offered both groups, blacks and women, the chance to stretch in ways they never had dreamed. To live away from family, as independent and vital individuals working as a team to win the war. To rise above the accepted, expected and narrow definitions of what was accessible to them. They moved to big cities, traveled overseas and fought a war, even if it was with a broom, or stenographer's pencil from behind a desk, or the wheel of a car, jeep or truck far behind the lines. Their world was forever changed, for the better. They would expect and demand more; change was coming. The cork once pulled from the Champagne bottle can never be replaced. So women gulped down the wine of freedom and possibility, of new responsibility and stretched their lives far beyond the restraints of Anniston, Alabama, Macon, Georgia, Valdosta or Gadsden.

My father was charming and sexually exciting, a Lieutenant quick to light the smoke of a young woman and always seemed to have a flask of whiskey to add to a cold 6-ounce coke in that greenish glass bottle cooled by blocks of ice in the Gulf station on the edge of every small southern town. After the recruiting talks came the night out of the stable for this married stud, a true breeding stallion, from the Grange Hall or a room in the county court house where his patriotic speech was given, a young lady would make it clear that she was available for a soda, dinner and then a drink and a roll in the hay.

How many half-brothers I have, I do not know. They must be out there, though, a half dozen or more, and now and then in an airport I walk by a doppelganger and we look at each other as looking in a mirror, keeping our histories and thoughts to ourselves. I imagine as we pass, glance, move apart, we both at the same time smile and shake our heads. I think of turning back but never do, just laugh a little out loud and go on going on.

Lt. Merrill always fucked up. Shot himself in the foot. Too

much whiskey, lack of self-control, lack of character and an endless need of ego stroking desire. The war was about him, not the soldiers dying in jungles, on beaches or in the cold. Not about the Jews dying by the millions, as did the Russians and the Japanese and so many others. It was about his conquests and sexual appetite and he ate often and broke many pieces of fine china along the way.

What happened is vague, but my guess is he seduced some general's wife or more likely a General's daughter and if she was underage, that would be no surprise either. Even being quite young would not be a surprise. There were often hints as to why we had to move from one neighborhood to another in and around Washington DC. People did not pick up and move during the post-World War II era. You could not move, for housing was so tough to come by, but we moved. My two grandfathers died, we came into money, and bought the house on Argyle Drive in Alexandria, Virginia.

But I imagine you do not go from the best job in the army recruiting females for the WAC, to training Negro troops in Virginia without having done some stupid and perverted act. I can see the General demanding that the culprit Lt. James W. Merrill, caught in bed or behind the shed with his daughter, some 16-year-old with her white dress off and his pants down, she getting hammered, him grinning charmingly. Or perhaps they were not caught in the act, but she got pregnant and told the truth about who the father was.

Of course, this story would happen again leading to the birth of my half-brother, David, when my Father made love to his brother's wife and got her pregnant. It was on purpose I suppose, to prove something petty and small, no doubt. My sense is this was not the first time he used his powers of persuasion, wealth, position and his privilege to score, take, use and abuse.

His life is marked by moments where he would step across lines of decency, race, and age as well as lines written in a law book, but those laws to this day are optional for the rich and well placed, and there is almost always a backdoor way out to keep the family name intact and their dirty reputation spotless.

My father trained Negro troops, which was about as far as one could fall from grace. He supposedly loved the job, at least the stories of how sharp and crisp they marched, their ability to bounce their white parade gun stocks off the street. They would grab them in midair as they spun around like James Brown singing *please, please*. They twirled them like batons, throwing them into the air and catching them without missing a beat or a step. He trained them to brush their teeth and these country boys learned to make a bunk so that a dime would bounce and flip over when dropped onto the blanket. He trained them to shoot, to march, to drive tanks and take pride in their unit. Most of these brilliant young black men would then march off to war to drive trucks, haul 55 gallon drums and leave their guns behind as they did the grunt work of keeping the front-line troops fed and supplied. It was a segregated army.

But Lt. Merrill took these assignments seriously and trained them and hung out with them, drinking corn whiskey and swapping stories. He made sure that his soldiers got the supplies, clothes, books and other army stuff they were promised. He made sure that they were well fed and to the best he could, in a racist world, tried to get them the respect that was automatically denied due to their color of skin.

At some point, he got drunk with them and fell off the back of a Sherman tank, busting his ribs and tearing up the lower lobe of his left lung, an injury that would fester for a decade until it nearly killed him. Again, being privileged saved his ass and in this case, his life. His connections got him into the National Institute of Health across from Walter Reed Hospital just outside of DC. There, he was one of the first men to have his lung removed. They took out the lower damaged lobe and he was not expected to live. But he was, if nothing else, tough and he beat the odds. He would never be physically the same after this massive operation in which they literally quartered him, no micro-surgery back in 1955, but with lots of tubes and stiches, somehow he made it back.

We had to move from the big house on Argyle Drive because

there were too many steps for him to get from the car to the house. So, we moved about two miles east to Fountain Street, across the street from a young Jim Morrison's house.

My father never returned to Anniston, Alabama or to the University of Alabama or to Auburn University. Why he had to leave the University of Alabama then leave Auburn were never part of the family story, meaning they were dark and to be kept there, unseen and if possible, unknown. He did things that were just not done, and got away with them, only leaving a wreck of lives and standards behind. He was in a top fraternity SAE, at the University; he was lined up to be a lawyer and a state representative. He married well and was on the curve to be another great Merrill but he ended up 1000 miles north in Washington DC. Why? What is the true story of James W. Merrill? So, Why? So many Whys? Looking back on his whole life it is not hard to guess what must have happened. It all came down to sex, ego, sex, ego and more sex. Perhaps a little gambling and a lot of whiskey and sex.

Decades after the war, as a big wig at the Agriculture Department in DC, he was in charge of peanuts in the Southeast and we would travel each summer from Alexandria, Virginia to Tampa, Florida then on through Alabama and drive home through the mountains of the Carolinas, returning after a month or so. On these trips, my mother, myself and my father stopped in small towns, the same ones he had traveled to as the good looking, sexy WAC recruiter. While my mother was reading to me in the park, always with its confederate statue facing south, my father would be giving a talk on peanut allotments and programs for growing grubbers in the same Grange Halls and county court houses where he had tempted young women to follow their new dreams and join the Women's Army Corp.

So, the physical memories of his past sexual conquest were there, all around us, the hotels, the restaurants, the road just outside of town, a good place to park in the dark, the grave yard or some other lovers leap. As we drove into the rural landscape of Georgia and Alabama he left these old towns with a grin and a half-told story that I did not get but my mother surely did.

Tar Baby

The shell hit in front of the rock wall that John Harper was using for protection. The force of the blast went through the wall, sheered-off a wedge of stone the size of a piece of cherry pie. Except the shard of flying rock was not soft or sweet but it was covered in deep red blood, imbedded in the Italian soil. The stone was sharp like flint tools, an edge as sharp as a scalpel. John was crouching, leaning his torso and head into the protective wall praying when the jagged piece flew into his inner thigh and crotch, cutting off one of his balls but not his cock.

His first reaction was that he had been spared and was not hit. The sound of the explosion stunned him, disoriented him and he lost sense of time, pain, place. Then he came back to reality, he felt the wetness of blood running down his leg. He looked down and could see a growing pool of blood directly between his legs. It took a moment more for him to realize he had been hit and was bleeding and then the reality struck him. The reality of *where* the projectile had struck him. He still felt no pain and he leaned his head or, more accurately, his helmet into the stonewall and simply said God no, God no. Looking deep into the surface of the rock squeezing his eyes shut, God No, he repeated. At last he reached between his legs and started to laugh and that is how the Sergeant found him grinning and laughing holding his undamaged cock in his right hand as blood dripped from his scrotum and inner thigh. The Sergeant said with a smile *should I put a tourniquet on that or just dress the wound* and they both laughed, perhaps the deepest and longest laugh of their short lives.

The pain came in waves as the medic re-dressed John's wound. It was not really all that bad, a four inch cut on the inner part of the thigh, the scrotum was sliced open, as if performed by a surgeon and one of his balls was hanging by a thread of tissue. The medic snipped it off, knowing it could not be saved, packed the leg wound and bandaged the scrotum. All the time talking to John, *well you're ok, you will be a father, most likely have a dozen kids with that one testicle. You're, really ok, you have not lost that much blood, and this will get you out of Italy. At least for a while.*

John would return to duty with his unit and fight in a number of engagements and get wounded two more times and save some of his men, he's got the medals to prove it, but like most soldiers who fought, he did not talk about it. So, the details did not filter down easily to his community in Alabama. Little talk of this injury was in his letters home.

Before the war he was a student at Auburn University and he was not sure of his interest but he was in a family that had attended Auburn for generations, so he was expected to go. Most likely to become a lawyer, but the war was what interested him, and he joined up as soon as he was brave enough to confront his father with that news. The family thought he would go to Officer's Candidate School, but he just wanted to be a soldier and fight, not lead, and so he ended up as a foot soldier in Africa, Sicily, and then Italy. In the front lines with a gun, not a pen and clipboard in his hand back in America, like my father. He was not without fear, but he had a deep belief in God and his life was in God's hands, so he relaxed in the danger of battle and was respected, if not loved by the men he served with. Many who would not return.

John was shy by nature, soft spoken and polite to a fault, not one to talk about himself. He was ordered to participate in an interview about his experiences on the battlefield and the medals he won. Where he was wounded was kept out of the article. It would not be good for morale, either in the front line or on the home front. The army needed heroes and he played a very reluctant part and was written about in Stars and Stripes. This got to his hometown newspaper, the Anniston Star, and he was designated a hero. With each telling of the story in his hometown his exploits grew. When he returned home, he was given an award from the mayor, introduced at public events and the country club held a John Harper celebration. He put up with it and was gracious. He knew that in time it would fade, and he focused on Lillian and their life. The story of having one nut cut off was kept a secret.

My father had known him since high school, and they were opposites. My father was swashbuckling, a braggart and brash; John was quiet and polite. John put others first, my father was first in all situations. My father craved the spotlight, he made sure it was on him.

But like many Southerners they had something in common, they both liked to drink. John liked to hear my father's stories of WWII as a recruiter of women for the WAC and a trainer of Colored Troops. This way, John did not have to talk about his war experience. Or the nightmares that he never spoke of. Around my father, John did not have to play the part of the hero others expected him to be. He was a friend and audience for the boastful and funny Jim Merrill. My father did not spend much time in Anniston after the war, for reasons unexplained he left the south and took a job in Washington DC, with the Department of Agriculture. He rose quickly to the top. Which was amazing because he knew nothing about farming and had no background in it. But he was clever, worked hard and understood power, so he was succeeding in spite of himself.

John came back and married his high school sweetheart, Lillian Sophie Remington and they settled down. John went to work for the state Agriculture Department in Anniston. Lillian, also called Sophie when she acted a little too serious, had worked as a nurse's assistant during the war and continued to help out at the clinic after they were married. But only three days a week. It was a volunteer assignment not a necessary 9 to 5 work-a-day job. Her place in society obligated her to schedule and attend important social obligations, including children's birthday parties and afternoon teas that had become important since the end of the war.

They joined the country club, attended the social engagements, and lived a good life. The years passed and it became clear to everyone that they were having trouble bringing a baby into the world. This became a topic of conversation and spread like a virus across their community. Perhaps it was Lillian's inability to have children or perhaps John's, the science was not sophisticated enough to tell them which. Perhaps it was John's wounded balls, one torn off in the explosion in Italy. In private, this is what he told her, that it was his fault and not hers. He was the one lacking, not Lillian.

They tried, but Lillian never got pregnant and they both wanted children. John, for reasons beyond the normal ones, like the love of fatherhood, family or the pressure of church and society. He had seen too much death in the war, including non-combatants, women and children, and he wanted to give a life of care and love to a child. Few people adopted in Anniston back then but they were sure about it and wanted a baby in the house and so they went to the adoption agency in Montgomery and did the paper work. Quicker than they had expected, there was an opportunity to adopt a baby. An infant with blue eyes and light brown hair, a beautiful child. An infant only days old left near the entrance of the hospital in Birmingham. They drove to see the beautiful blued-eyed child. So, small and delicate, a boy, so perfect and so all alone in the world. A child too young to have a memory of a past life, of a first mother or father. The child was a gift from God and so perfect. The adoption went through quickly, power and place allowed the strings to be pulled, pressure and favors applied to get the Harpers this baby. Almost overnight they were parents and they were good at it.

By the time the baby was three, it was clear he was mixed race, by four it was the worst of all possibilities, he was mixed white and Negro. The problems Lillian and John faced were insurmountable. The only choice was to give up their boy and try to get a new kid. Their boy could not go to kindergarten, or any of the public or private all-white schools, he could not swim or play at the country club. Negros were not allowed, even the son of a war hero and well-to-do member of the community. He could not even swim at the public pool. Soon, taking the child to the movie would be impossible. The seating was segregated, and blacks sat in the balcony and whites down stairs.

This was not a mestizo's culture where there were many levels of mixed races, each combination with different rights, accesses and possibilities, differing degrees of social acceptance. Here in

Alabama and in the old confederate states things were either black or white, people were either black or white. One drop of Negro blood and you were doomed to inferior status and nothing could be done to change this reality. The choice was clear, you either got rid of the baby you had loved for four years and gave him to a black family to live under the brutal southern apartheid culture or you moved north. Moving north to live excommunicated from their families, community, hometown, memories, and heritage was, for them, also not a possibility.

The choice for Lillian Sophie Remington and John was an impossible choice. They could not give up this child they had so learned to love, a child that had become a part of them. They could not simply say *well, he is a Negro and so you all take him to the other side of the tracks*. They were told by friends and family he must go, for his own good. John and Lillian could not leave little Jacob to grow up in the restricted world applied to Negros, with its lack of education, careers, inability to buy a house in a "good neighborhood". They could not imagine Jacob not going to swim in the pool at the country club with the other children, have to always travel in the back of the bus, not get a cold shake at the soda fountain on Main Street, and on and on. They could not accept this life sentence for their son. Nor could they simply leave their families, friends, church, schools, social circles behind them. So, they suffered and did nothing.

They did not have to make a decision, for it was quickly made for them. The country club made it clear they were not welcome on their grounds with their son and soon they got a letter saying it was best not to come down to the club. Their membership was not renewed. John was replaced in his golf foursome and they were no longer invited to bridge parties. Their families asked them not to bring Jacob over, *no need to get his hopes up of belonging to the family* was often repeated. He was not allowed to go to kindergarten anymore and he was miserable at being left out of activities with his former playmates.

My father called John and offered him a position at the Department of Agriculture in DC. He told him that Jacob, now 5, would be able to go to integrated schools soon in

Arlington, Virginia, the county right next to Alexandria where we lived. Houses were expensive $15,000 and up, but it was very possible. The community was made up of many new families, moving to Washington from all over the country and many were in the military. This was important because the military had now been integrated for 10 years. Northern Virginia was moving beyond the South's Massive Resistance to Brown Verses Topeka and beginning to open the school doors, if just a crack, for colored children. And they were doing it without the mobs and racial terror of Little Rock. Here John and Lillian would have a chance to love their Negro son, their mixed-race boy. Raise him in a community that was arcing toward integration and rights of public access. But even here it would not be pleasant. The north was a haven, but not a heaven for mixed-race and colored folks.

John and Lillian and little Jacob moved and moved quickly, getting first an apartment and then buying a house. No one asked about the race of their child when they signed the papers on their new home. What people thought in the neighborhood they moved into was a different matter. How people acted toward John, Lillian and Jacob would be a broad spectrum from support, kindness to outright hate. Most simply kept their distance.

When Lillian went to say good-bye to her family in Anniston, her grandfather met her at the door. Knowing that they were leaving the next day, he could not stop himself from inflicting as much damage as possible. He opened the door and blurted out *where that nigger baby of yours, you ain't bringing that nigger baby in here is ya?* She took a deep breath and steadied herself to overcome her fear, anger and deep sadness. *No Big Daddy, Jacob is not with me and I will not be bringing him here today.* The old man growled, *Well, not today or any day* and then took a deep drag off his cigarette. He stood menacingly blocking the door, Lillian's sister Martha Jane, came and Big Daddy stepped aside, tottered away, smoking hard, to sit in his chair in his living room.

We visited the Harpers several times. I must have been six or seven years old. They never visited us. I guess our property, our house, was restricted. I remember the visits, the parents did what parents do, sat in the living room or on a porch and talked politics and drank. My father being the main act, the entertainment. Whether they liked the show or not he always put one on. Jacob and I were sent to play in his bedroom, we always stayed inside even on nice days. All of this was normal to me at the time. Even though I wanted to go out in the yard and play, I was told not today, best to stay inside. I though nothing more of it.

It was only seen as a pattern related to race, fear and non-acceptance much later. I did notice Jacob was different than the rest of my friends. His skin was slightly darker, a coffee with lots of cream color. His lips full and he had wavy hair with a kink to it. No one else I played with on our block or at school looked this way. Joel Cohen had dark eyes and dark wavy hair but not kinky and his Mother looked the same. The Whites were blondes and so were the Stevens. Irene, my Negro nanny, had kinky hair, kind of like Jacob's but he was much lighter than she was. No one informed me about Jacob's internal racial divide, but I knew that kids like him did not stay in the motels we stayed in, they did not swim in our pools or go to our school.

I could see with my own eyes, he was different and something told me that his difference made him less, reduced his status, diminished him as a person. His life was not a bargain, but it would be cut-rate, decreased and low-priced, but no bargain. Like Irene, the maid and nanny that took care of me, the person I trusted deeply, she was somehow less for being colored. I could see it in the ratty house she lived in, the shoeless kids running around their yard, a yard without grass, a house in the bad section of town, the Negro area, the poor section.

Irene had to catch a bus to work in our house, she did not drive. When we sometimes had to take her home and she did not ride in the front seat next to my mother or father. She was placed in the back. The fact that this made my parents chauffeurs did not seem to pass into their consciousness. They saw letting a Negro ride in the front seat with them as a symbol. It raised their value to a level nearing equality. But placed in the back seat, the Negro passenger was safely in their place. Safely on the back of the bus.

The reality of the value of dark skin was made clear in so many ways. It did not have to be clarified, there was no need for an explanation because it was demonstrated daily by all aspects of society. We were white folks and they were black, and the society raised one up and lessened the other. It was impossible to not experience this truth. When you are inside that society, when it is your heritage, you do not question obvious injustices. You do not question what you cannot see. It takes time and effort to see the world anew and it means destroying the old world: the one you grew up in and loved.

I treated Jacob like any other friend I played with, asked no questions of my parents about Jacob's skin, hair, or his lips. The times we visited and played, always inside, we had fun and these questions disappeared. Our interest was in our imaginations our childhood games and interests. He was just a kid I played with because my parents visited their family four or five times a year.

My father would lecture us on the drive over to visit the Harpers about what a hero John was. How he never talked about the war and that was the way it went with the real men who fought in WWII. If a G.I. bragged about his fighting in the war, he was a liar and a fraud. *You could bet on that.* John Harper never spoke about this heroism and my father's lecture continued like a street preacher on a soap box. What my mother and father did not bring up was the real bravery John Harper and his wife, Lillian, demonstrated. Their heroism was an everyday action. It was heroic to love and raise a mixed-race adopted child, make a Negro child their own. The fact, that he was accepted as inseparable from them was a miracle. Jacob was one with them, as inseparable, and unconditionally loved as a natural born child and perhaps a bit more.

What is the end of this story? What happened to Jacob and his parents? Why did they slip from my family's life? Why were they no longer friends and never spoken of again? Well, it was not discussed or bragged about. But small bits slipped out.

Lillian and John needed to return to Anniston, Alabama for a funeral and knew they could not take Jacob. They were sure my parents would take him in for a week while they drove and returned from the deep south. Their trusted friends, my parents, stabbed them in the back with a knife so hard it plunged directly into their hearts. My parents simply said *no, we cannot have a Negro boy living with us, that would not do*. It would cause trouble. John and Lillian had run into the same hatred in Anniston. The hatred that had driven them north. Now the very people that had been so generous to help them escape and start a new life, were in the end no different from those they had left in Alabama. Those that they still loved in Alabama, from them they expected such behavior. But no! not the Merrill's, they knew better, they were friends. They would not treat Jacob as less because he was mixed-race. But Jim and Evelyn Merrill could not cross that bridge, Jacob was not a white child with those innate privileges, so they let the Harpers down. Only one of them headed south for the funeral. The other stayed and cared for Jacob. In the end, the Harpers disappeared from our life and memory. I never played in Jacob's room again.

Field Hands

It would be decades before I understood why, as a 13-year-old, I stood in the middle of a peanut field in Georgia. I stood there with my parents over 55 years ago and today can still recall it. But I recall it through an older man's memory, eyes and insight. We stood next to a home, really just a run-down shack but still a home, a home for a family, a family of Negros in 1950's parlance, a family of poor sharecroppers. I had seen these homes, these tumble down shacks in the middle of sun baked fields often. I looked at them from the comfort of the back seat of our Packard. I saw these poor folks each summer of my childhood as my family tooled down two lane roads heading from Washington D.C. to Anniston, Alabama. Yes, I had seen them as we flew by. I knew they were sharecroppers and that my father was in charge of peanuts for the federal government, a big wig position at the Department of Agriculture. He drank toddies of old crow poured into 6-ounce coke bottles as he lectured my mother and me about peanuts, farmers, sharecropping, politics and his inflated view of himself. We drove along at 45 miles an hour, if we were lucky. My mother and I were merely passengers for my father's self-aggrandizing stories. He was on this annual summer speaking tour of small southern towns where he would give planters the low down on annual peanut allotments.

This sharecropper's home sat in the middle of a field, surrounded by hard punished red dirt and windblown sand, not a blade of grass grew there. I stood in front of the house, a home they made in a shot-gun shack they did not own, but could not leave. It was a one-story rectangle with a front porch and three rooms suspended on cement blocks about two feet off the red Georgia clay. The front porch was thankfully shaded by a rusted corrugated tin roof sheltering two open windows, the screens long ago blown out and the front door sighted in between. As I looked in, I looked right back out. The front door was perfectly lined up with the back door and you looked straight through the structure. In fact it did not have rooms as I knew them, with walls and individual doors. The interior was more or less divided into three small areas, a living dining room in front, beds in the next small section and in the back was a pantry and kitchen that tumbled out into the field.

One did not have to enter the structure of old lumber and rusted tin to take all this in. A simple glance through the open front door told you the complete layout of the house. The front door in fact was on the ground in front of the place making a sort of walkway to the three steps up to the front porch. A bridge for safe passage during the often occurring afternoon thunderstorms. There were well used chairs on the porch but no one was sitting, a wash tub and scrub board hung neatly on the wall next to a colorful hand painted sign Mr. Rainy, as he was introduced to me by my father, must have carefully made. He had named his family home *Shack-ri-La* which made no sense to me at all as I stood there that afternoon but I would get the wonderful literary joke he made in a dream decades later. In my thirties, I would wake laughing to my wife's amazement that anyone could wake from a deep sleep in utter laughter.

But that day we were not in Shangri La, but a field of peanuts with sweat dripping down my face as I looked through the open door, took in the house, the fields, the children living there, Mr. Halbert Rainy and his wife Iness. For God knows what reason I imagined this place in a thunderstorm, rain pouring down in buckets forming a huge brown muddy lake engulfing this little wood and corrugated house sitting up on its cement blocks. It would have looked like a poor man's Noah's Ark. An ark for the scrawny yard bird chickens running about, the half-nude shoeless children, their mother and Mr. Rainy, who was warmly speaking with my father. I, for an instance, imagined us all caught in this storm, a downpour, all running into their home through the un-closable front door, all together as one inside the leaking structure. Rain pouring down with deafening percussion, like a cow pissing on a tin roof, as my father use to say, the two families together laughing under the leaking rusted roof and waiting. Waiting for the rain to stop.

I was roused from my fantasy by the rustle and giggling of the

Rainy children, standing bare foot, and like me their sweat dripped down their faces, leaving traces like tiger stripes on their dark, dust covered cheeks. I wondered if I looked the same to them as they did to me? We stood staring at each other sweating and grinning, uneasy, curious, happy, and unsure. But most of all quiet and polite, for we existed as background figures in a play in which we had no speaking part.

Looking back, it is now obvious that my father knew this man and knew Halbert Rainy well, for they shook hands and talked warmly. These two men, who could not sit in public together, were friends. Who were only separated by custom, Jim Crow laws, and color, separated by the deep hatred that lay just below the surface of southern society. Two men separated by education, access, economics and dress stood grinning, shaking hands, unaware for that moment of what was around them. They were lost deeply in each other's caring grasp. They were lost in some memory, existing someplace else, where their bond was first cemented. Their difference so obvious to my mother, to his wife, to his children and to me, was for that moment non-existent for the two of them. There were just two men who were deeply glad to see each other.

The rows of peanuts stretched away from the little house and ended at the tree line bordering the field on three sides. The dirt road we drove in on stretched out behind us, back to the two-lane rural highway. Rows of grubbers struggled to grow on both sides of this dirt track, most were bent over and brown, seemingly dying of thirst in the August southern sun.

My mother, once a debutant, stood by the car, very uncomfortable in the heat. As I look back, she was no doubt made much more uncomfortable by her sense of what was polite, appropriate and right more than the oppressive heat and humidity. Standing in this field of poverty, with a Negro family was crossing the line of separation she had grown up with and accepted was making her uneasy. So was seeing the depth of this poverty, it was a forced realization of truth. The truth of one family, of individual folks with real eyes, noses and smiles. People that she now was vaguely connected to by standing in their "front yard". Seeing this family no longer as a group of Negros out working in a filed at a distance but as people standing in front of their home, as a family living in a world of such disadvantage, work and pain wrenched her insides and made her feel faint. She leaned back against the car and became frightened by the eyes of the children and their mother staring at her but they were in fact looking past her, marveling at my family's brand new three-toned pink and white 1956 Packard Clipper. It had been purchased from a company that would be out of business at the end of that year. Another "good" decision made by my parents, just one among many.

The sun beat us down, and there were no cold drinks, certainly not, they had no electricity or ice. They had no cool drinks, no cool breeze, no sweet summer shade. They did have had-a-call and beans, the relentless sun, buzzing flies, the silver moon lit nights filled with mosquitoes, hot endless summer days of work and cold winters of work if they could find it, not much more.

I stood near the broke down front door and looked past the eyes of children my age and younger to see the rough board walls some covered with plaster others with old newspapers, it struck me as amazing to have newspapers on the walls. From floor to ceiling, old newspapers, whose pattern was broken by an occasional poster or advertisement printed on thicker cardboard. This great modernist art collage, glued to the walls, was sharecropper insulation. It was not art, but it was creative in a different way: it was there to fill the spaces between the rough cut wooden boards, there to keep the bugs, cold and wind out. It was there because the man that built this house loved his wife and kids, and in time it would be plastered over if he had a good crop and a little extra money come fall.

We drove away, windows up, keeping the cloud of dust the Packard kicked up on the outside and the cigarette smoke, smell of whiskey and heat inside. At the turn of the dirt track and the gravel two lane was a brick one story building with six green doors and six small open windows. The parking lot was filled with old cars and black men and women sitting on a bench under an oak tree. The men and women were sitting in the only bit of shade near the parking area. They fanned themselves and talked, watched us drive up and turn. The rooms they had rented must have been like ovens. A hand painted sign suspended from the wooden electric pole spelled out MOTEL.

This motel was an oasis, a shelter in a segregated world. Our motels, the one we easily found nightly as we drove south, were always under the shade of beautiful lush pine trees. The sunlight through the pines always casting a beautiful web of shadows over the property during the day, except for the area for the swimming pool. The pools were small but fun and not always cool but at least blue and inviting. The trees around our motels had their trunks painted white up to about six feet high and car tires had been cut in half and also painted white. These were used as decorative borders for the pine tree park in front of the motels with their picnic tables and old-style iron swings and slides for younger children.

There was always a small diner nearby with several tables covered in cotton tablecloths. On the tables were sugar cubes in a bowl, always a pre-dinner snack of sublime sweetness. The diners served fried foods and cold drinks, actual drinks with ice, a luxury in 1950's.

I wanted to get back to our motel to swim. The disparity that surrounded me was normal, uncomfortable but still normal and my life was secured by another set of rules, another world, I just wanted to get to my motel and swim. The children I left behind were no more a concern than a squirrel running up a tree or a bird landing on a branch. They just were as I was, life as experienced by a self-concerned 13 year old.

We sat for a moment in the three-toned pink Packard and looked at the Negro motel sweltering in the dusty heat and a sun that still would not set for hours. Then we turned perhaps left or perhaps right and headed toward comfort and a good meal, a swim and for my parents: more cocktails, to be drunk under the buzz of neon lights, not the buzz of pesky mosquitoes. Those mean bugs were kept at bay by doses of mosquito insecticide provided by trucks with DDT delivered as a fog-like gas. The fog spread around the motels like some vision from a WWI battlefield. I chased after the trucks, playing war. The fog of

DDT quickly dispersed. The deep blue twilight sky was turning black and a lovely, bug-free evening lay ahead.

Years later, as I now sit in my study and try and write about my life, the reality of the situation becomes clear. My father had trained black troops during World War II and often spoke with great pride of the men he trained and how they had ended up fighting in the front line in Italy and were real heroes. He did not go with them. Perhaps he could have, but he was married with kids, and the son of a powerful man, so he did not have to go. Was Halbert Rainy one of the troops he trained? Did he survive the war against Nazi race supremacy only to come home to Georgia and face again the South's white race supremacy? As I look back, he was literate, perhaps very well read, and he should have been in University. You could tell by his hand painted sign *Shack-ri-La* this guy was special, knew some things but for reasons we can all attest to this future was not open to him. The army, the war, his literacy, his hoped for future were derailed by someone owing the boss man more than can be made in a peanut field, perhaps a newly pregnant wife after his return and other stresses led him back into this field of servitude. It had to all be connected, the respect between this white man and this black man was real but kindness and benevolence does not change injustice and on this road toward the future the two men walked in opposite directions.

That Good Old Off Broadway Play

The Zenith Cobra console radio and turntable was a major piece of furniture in the Stevens' living room, taking up a good part of one wall. The Cobra, with its shining maple top, also held a large blue glass ashtray, a lamp and pink elephant coasters waiting for cold cocktails. The radio could be tuned to an AM Station, FM was small time in 1957, or tuned to short wave or a marine band which was a series of noises like Morse code. Tonight, for the neighborhood cocktail party, the Cobra played *Seventy-six trombones led the big parade with a hundred and ten cornets close at hand...*from the very popular Broadway play *Music Man.*

Everyone in the room knew the plot for the Music Man, of the trickster, Professor Harold Hill, a scam artist, who would sell the folks of River City, Iowa, band instruments and uniforms, then skip town with their money. My mother and father, like all the folks on the block, had not seen the play but had read all about the Broadway hit and loved the music. Loved the music of Meredith Wilson, Lerner and Loewe, and Rodgers and Hammerstein. These songs from musical theatre were the top 40 of their era: sophisticated music and lyrics for sophisticated people.

Argyle Drive, the cul-de-sac on which we lived, was a neighborhood for the best and the brightest. The Barns were from New England. Both Ira and Elaine had attended Ivy League universities and were doctors and scientists. Next door, the Whites were German-American. Richard White worked for the World Bank, the family had traveled extensively in India and Pakistan. They were deeply involved in helping these poor countries after WWII. They had brought over a German orphan, a 16 year old Jan, to give him a new start in America.

Next to them and the host of the party were the Stevens, both husband and wife were some type of writers and their house was a library, like a public library but without the quiet. They had five kids and the place was a wonderful chaotic riot of a family and home.

Next to them were the Cohens, a Jewish family that ran a haberdashers Cohen's Quality Shop, one of the best men's clothing stores in Alexandria or even Washington for that matter. I used to be taken there twice a year to be measured for suits. Each September, for a dark suit and at Easter for a sear sucker or other light-colored summer suit. The Cohens had brought over several distant relatives from Germany or Poland who had somehow survived the Nazi extermination camps. When the kids from the block played or went to see our friends Joel and Neil Cohen we had to be very, very, quiet so as to not disturb these ghosts, for that is what these survivors were. We knew they were in the house and we had all seen on TV the images of the dead bodies being buried in trenches, pushed in by bull dozers. We knew they were in the house, but we did not see them often, but the few times we did see them, a man and a woman, at the end of a dark hallway, staring out at us through their broken minds, a little bent over and very frightened. Moving like ghosts through their doors into their room: vanished.

These were bright people on Argyle Drive, with PHD's, master's degrees, successful in life, with their families, with their professions and they were politically active. Everyone who attended the cocktail parties were progressives, liberal supporters of FDR styled programming, future supporters of John Kennedy and the New Frontier. The Barns, Stevens and Whites were involved in fighting for Civil Rights and Voting Rights for Negros. They had written letters, signed petitions, marched, joined the NAACP and protested for the integration of school in Northern Virginia. They were brave and considerate.

All of this is the opposite of my parent's values and culture. They were go-slow progressive Southerners, who knew change was coming, even supported it, in a very vague way, but could not see living next to a Negro, or having their children in schools with "them". Equality was an abstraction, sustaining the system, the heritage, and the southern culture was of higher value than giving people of color their legal and constitutional rights. They hated the racial violence, the terror of the KKK and other lower bottom feeding scum. Yet they knew it was not some small radical minority that led to the lynchings and racial terror in the South. They repeated the northern myths, the myths that they knew from their own family heritage were not true. My father's own family was involved in lynchings and would be involved with the Klan less than ten years in the future.

In my father's position at the top of the Department of Agriculture, he had helped black farmers and sharecroppers, often did the right and moral thing, the good thing, he saw himself as good, he had stormed out of a Baptist church service with family in tow after the minister damned Negros as the children of Cain, marked for life as inferior and sinful. In reality, he was a man with a plantation mentality, where equality was not based in law but on individual benevolence. He was benevolent towards the Negro race and toward the poor.

Benevolence is not equality, it is superiority, the right to be kind or not to be fair. It is the fundamental right of the privileged, the power given to the giver for throwing scraps to the poor. In this system, the position of the Negro, the underclass, does not change, for the power dynamic has not been adjusted. My father did not hate a person because of the color of their skin, in fact he was more than willing to get in bed with *colored girls* but was not about to allow them to take their place as his equal. They were never to be introduced as a girlfriend, even a friend or a mistress. How many brothers of color do I have? There is most likely at least one in an era of no birth control, well, I do not know, but...

My father's discussions with the neighbors on race always turned to ugly arguments, then got really nasty and personal at the parties on Argyle Drive. My father would take any attack on the Southern system as a personal attack on himself and respond with anger and bitterness. My Mother defended his outrageous behavior to us, his children and seemed proud of his threat to take the argument outside. To us, she said, he was being bullied and they were picking on him, goading him on. His flawed position, articulated while drunk, was not considered. It was the Northerner's fault, they did not understand the *Negro Problem* as Southerners did.

So, the Whites, Stevens, Barns and Cohens had talked and decided it was best not to talk about race or civil rights at all during the next block cocktail party, at least as long as my mother and father were there. Keep it light, was the plan, let's just be kind and have some fun.

All went well in the beginning, the adults dressed in light casual wear, the women in dresses and the men in slacks and Hawaiian shirts. The Cobra played show tunes, people swayed to the music while waiting for mixed drinks from the bar. Drinks with silly umbrellas and swizzle sticks were handed out on funny party napkins and of course trays of snacks: hot dog pieces wrapped in bacon, Swedish meatballs and other goodies from the 1950's Good Housekeeping cookbook.

My Father, already half-wasted before arriving, before walking down our steps and across the street, was spoiling for a fight. To not talk about civil rights in 1957 was difficult but in the first two weeks of September it was impossible. The neighbors did not bring up the subject but my father did. How could you avoid the question or not give an honest response?

My father walked in, got his drink, walked over to Bill Stevens, did not say *hi* or *how are things* but enquired *What do you think about this business down in Little Rock, about those nine colored kids who are attempting to go to that all-white high school?* Without a pause, he went on *What do you think of that rascal Governor Faubus, calling out the Arkansas National Guard to block the school from those nine nicely dressed Negro kids?*

Stevens was trapped, and could not side step the questions, that had been laid out to start an argument and Bill Stewart's sense of justice got the best of him, he took the bait and an argument erupted on race and civil rights, all in the first ten minutes of the party. Well, the best laid plans and all that. Bill responded with all his might and indignation. He, as all who had a heart, were deeply moved by the story and images from Arkansas.

The images on the front page of the Washington Post were heart-stopping, for Southerners, as well as Northerners, whether you were for *separate but equal* or for integration, the images were heartbreaking. Both sides asked themselves *could this be America? My parents asked, *could this be the Southern culture that raised me?* That I am part of, and love? Like the brutal images of the white mobs screaming and spitting on colored children, the truth, the truth they found in their hearts was a brutal affirmation of a deep-seated hatred in their society. These amazing images of nine colored children, keeping their composure and dignity while white folks went berserk, made it obvious that just below the surface of the genteel, gentle, gracious South was a boiling pot of uncontrolled racial terror. Racial terror that matched the passions of German Nazis.

It was undeniable and this time the hatred could not be blamed on a few, the scum that supposedly made up the Klan, because these were everyday folks, good law-abiding, kind, religious Southerners. They were too close to my mother and father, who had been brought up buying the pack of lies behind separation and racial inequality. They now hurt deeply and what they saw could only be defended with insane loops and twists of logic. They rode those loops and attempted to justify what they knew to be unjust. They looked past the ugly faces of screaming white people to the likelihood of invasion of a state by the Federal Government, with our United States Army. This was, to them, the real crime.

Bill Stewart spoke faster and with more anger than he wished too, *did you see the faces of those people, spitting and yelling at those poor colored children, it is beyond disgraceful, it is hatred and nothing but ignorant hatred. Think of it, the Governor bringing in the State National Guard troops to prevent a handful of kids from attending a school, purposely enflaming the situation, letting that white mob know that they are in power and will not be punished for what they do. How can you sit there and support those folks and there, there, Governor. It is beyond understanding.*

My father, unsteady in his chair, not able to decide to stand, attack, or sit, blurted out, *and if President Eisenhower brings in the 101 Airborne, invades the south with the American army to force integration of a high school, it will get much worse, we could have another War Between the States on our hands. People have a right to defend themselves, their values, culture and heritage and people in Little Rock have rights too, what about their rights?*

Nonsense came a chorus of voices, *Your states have had their opportunity to make right by the people they used to own, former slaves. What have you done to better the lives of these people, these Negros? Name one law in the south, in your state of Alabama, you have told us your father was Lt. Governor, what did he do to help these poor people!*

We have accomplished more than you all will ever know and it was not on the front page of the Washington Post or the New York Times. We Southerners have made strides in race relations. I have met George Washington Carver, he changed agriculture in the South and far beyond. His ideas were not developed at Harvard or Yale but at Tuskegee University in Alabama and that is one of the first institutions of higher learning for Negros in America, North or South. He loves the South and told Negros to stay not go North to the ghettos in your part of the county. To stay and to build their life in Alabama to 'Put your bucket down.' That was the last phrase he got out of his mouth before a cascade of criticism poured down and he was forced to sit, mouth open pointing and taking it.

The Cohens, the Barns, the Whites, the Heffners and even the Beers, an older quiet and kind couple piled in. My father must have looked like Bruce Lee fighting off a hundred ninjas in movies decades later. He was reduced to half-sentences and noises, he tried to shout out all the old argument, he repeated, swerved from one attacker to the next.

There was no case law behind the Supreme Court decision in Brown verses Topeka. It will not stand... You people in the north do not really know Negroes and have no knowledge of how to live next to them... Have you lived in a tent with Negro boys, well I have...I have trained colored troops and understood what they needed...The

South is changing but it must come from the local level, the state, not imposed by the federal government...Sending troops is an invasion of America by the Federal Government...

Nothing like this has happened since the reconstruction...Mixing races, mixing blood, will be the end of culture as we know it...Look at your industrial cities, Harlem or Detroit, even here in Washington...

He continued to fight back, questions coming in torrents, from all sides and in the background the Music Man recording being playing on the Zenith Cobra was drowned out. It was an odd mixture of musical happiness, casually dressed men and women, and the bitterness of the divide between Americans. Nathan Cohen sat with his wife, smoking and listening, looking at the front page of the Washington Post with photographs of the mob yelling at the students in Little Rock. Cohen usually did not venture into the political conversations with the PhD's and his highly educated neighbors. He thought about the ghosts in his house and spoke loudly so as to get the attention of his wife seated right next to him on the sofa. His eastern European accent filled the room, as he put out his cigarette, *is this what they looked like?*

Everyone stopped interrupting each other and looked at Nathan and listened. When he saw that he had the floor he was a bit embarrassed, *What, what do I know, I know nothing, but I do know this, that the faces of the people in Arkansas, the people here on the front page of this newspaper are the faces of Kristallnacht.* He held the paper up and shook it. *I have known those faces and I see where they lead.*

He was cut off by my father. He lost it, yelling at his neighbors, *This is not Germany in 1939, that cannot happen here, that comparison is not fair. We fought for "your" people in Europe and many a Southern boy died, black and white, died for freedom.* The dam had broken and the flood of abuse poured down on my father, more comparisons to WWII and Nazis, voting, stealing land, incarceration, keeping negroes under-educated, fear of mixed marriages, lynching, the litany went on and on.

Mrs. White got up looked at the pile of albums and smiled. No one was sure how long ago the Music Man album had reached its end and the only sound coming out of the mono-speakers was the spiral of fuzz and clicks at the end of the vinyl after the music had passed. She looked thoughtfully at the pile of albums and choose South Pacific. She carefully put the needle down on the 5th selection on the album. She had to eyeball the placement of the needle and got just the end of the 4ᵗʰ selection *Nothing like a Dame*, a snappy tune, that made everyone look toward the Cobra console to see what was going on. For the first time in 30 minutes people were really quiet, exhausted. Their emotions and passions from the fight had rung the energy out of everyone and the room was filled with the beauty of music. A sad and slow tune began: *You've got to be taught (carefully taught).*

Everyone listened, embarrassed by their own passion and that perhaps that they had knocked down one too many. The words from the speakers of the Cobra floated through the evening darkness. The words floated in the air and all listened, not making a noise.

You've got to be taught (carefully taught)
To hate and fear,
You've got to be taught
From year to year,
It's got to be drummed
In your dear little ear
You've got to be carefully taught.
You've got to be taught to be afraid
Of people whose eyes are oddly made,
And people whose skin is a diff'rent shade,
You've got to be carefully taught.
You've got to be taught before it's too late,
Before you are six or seven or eight,
To hate all the people your relatives hate,
You've got to be carefully taught!

I am through with you people! my father said in a low voice as the tune ended. He slammed down his newly poured drink of coke and Four Roses. *I have never seen such a group of hypocrites!* His voice rose, exhausting the exhausted people, *You all say you care for Negroes, you seem to know what is best for me, for them, the*

South, and more. But look at you, do not know any NEGROES!?, I do and perhaps one day you will and you will see what fools you have been. Evelyn, let's go.

The for-sale sign went up in our front yard early the next week, people called feeling guilty for having forced us to move, but glad we were going, guilt and victory go together in America and perhaps elsewhere. Like Professor Harold Hill in the Music Man, though, my father had devised a scheme for the ages. He would not get the town's money, but he would get revenge and prove a point that was best left unproven. Like most acts of hate, it is others that are hit by the blunt force of the actions, in this case that included his wife and children and a family of unwitting strangers.

The sign was up for about two weeks and several people showed up and looked at our house perched on top of the hill looking down on the rest of the cul-de-sac. Then in the second week of October, a flashy Cadillac pulled up and parked at the curb outside the house. The couple got out and looked across the neighborhood, many of the neighbors were out cutting their grass with push mowers, children were playing in the street, throwing Frisbees, a new space age toy, boys and girls swaying, laughing and spinning hula hoops around their waists. All stopped and looked suspiciously at the car and the couple looking back and smiling at them. The Whites were raking some early fall leaves into a pile in the street, soon the air in Alexandria would be a wonderful haze with the smell from burning oak and maple leaves. The burning of leaves was a social ritual bringing everyone into their yards on fall Saturday and Sunday afternoons. Most everyone on Argyle Drive was in their yard as expected this Saturday afternoon, enjoying the Indian Summer, the golden glow of fall.

They watched as the couple dressed in their Sunday best climbed the front stairs, up the two-terraced hill to the Merrill's front porch, walked right up to the door and knocked. Jim Merrill opened the door lavishly and invited the well dressed, middle-aged Negro couple in. He looked out across the block to see that the neighbors were watching and be sure they had seen them.

The couple was invited to sit in the living room, this of course was a first, to have Negroes sitting on our couch. It was all terribly uncomfortable, and my father sat in his chair looking at his guests. They were feeling deadly awkward in his living room. A man that they did not really know and had never been in his house prior to this piece of theatre. He offered them a drink of whiskey, which they turned down, but not my father, he got up and got his drink and came back. With the whiskey taking its effect he started telling stories, became himself, making the couple laugh and the gentleman, with his Sunday suit, said he would like to take that drink after all. His wife groaned in disbelief. My father went into his lecture on race and his audience, nodded in agreement. Saying an occasional *Yes sir, I see your point. Yes sir, you is right*, time slipped by. A second drink was poured.

Who were these folks? How did my father know them? Was it a family he had helped, maintenance men at work in the basement of the Agriculture Department, professionals perhaps, lawyers in the Negro Community that had needed my father's help for God knows what reason? This mystery would go unsolved. Where was my mother? Sick in bed, she had been sick for about a week, I now look back and imagine the stress, a mini nervous breakdown from having to sell the house and destroying her fragile friendships with our neighbors. She did not care to move and had no say in any of it.

The trap was set and this mean-spirited southern imitation of Professor Harold Hill was playing his part perfectly, as did the rest of the cast. He opened the front door and stood on the front porch with the couple for a little too long. The neighbors watched, as my father and the Negros shook hands, lavishly, he then walked the couple down the stairs to their car. They shook hands again and the couple got in and waved. As they drove to the top of the circle and turned the Cadillac in a wide arc allowing everyone on the cul-de-sac a grand view of the wealthy Negros in the Cadillac, then they headed back down the hill. My father waved and smiled at the neighbors, climbed up the hill to our house and went in only to come out and descend the stairs to the for-sale sign and paste on it a large red sticker that said *SOLD*. Looking at it with pride, he waved to everyone, climbed the stairs to the house, went in and sat in his chair next to the phone.

Our phone did not ring till later that evening but all the other phones in the block were ringing off the hooks. The Merrill's sold their house and it looked as if a colored family purchased it. Our phone rang right at 7:00. Dinner was from 5:30 to 6:30 and no one called on the phone at that time. It was not polite. The call came from Janice White, saying that everyone on the block had questions about who our new neighbors were. My father said gleefully *Yes, I sold the house to the Washington's and they have six kids.* Jan White paused and chocked a little, *six children?*

Yes, at least, my father laughed, *and lots of cousins and aunts, it is a really nice, BIG family. I am sure you will love them.* Jan responded, *Like I said, people are interested in knowing about them, would you like to come to the Stevens' and have a drink and tell us about them, it is kind of a block meeting.*

The time was set for 8:15, at the Stevens' home, in the same room where the skirmish had begun, but this time the Cobra did not spin any discs, there was no music tonight. Everyone was on edge and my father entered, my mother would not go with him. She could not stand to watch the loss of her friends, and most likely knew nothing of his plans till it unraveled that Saturday in October.

Well, Jim, we understand that you sold the house, congratulations, but mmmm, let me ask mmm if it was to the couple we saw today, the Negro couple.

Why, yes, I thought you would be delighted to have Negro neighbors.

Mr. Barn's thought and said very carefully, *Yes, we do not mind, do not mind at all, not at all having Negro neighbor's... and one day we hope to... but right now is not the time... not everyone in the area feels the way we do. There are many on the adjoining streets that would be very upset about it. We have all talked and do not believe that this is the right time to do this, to sell to a Negro family.*

Why not! You want them in your schools, you want them to vote, to have access to the public pool and the hotels you stay in? These are your words, you want them to have access to restaurants, and all public accommodations. This is what you have been telling me every chance you get. But now you do not want to live next to "them"! Do I understand or am I missing something???

Look, White said, *I am sure they are a very wonderful family, but it is not that simple, we have to think about the values of our homes, our responsibility to the broader neighborhood and the values of their homes, and much more. Where will their kids be going to school, our schools in the district have yet to integrate. While it is something we support, we do not have control of these aspects of the situation. We have to take in account others views and beliefs. Is living here even fair to them?*

They looked at my father but for once he said nothing, just sat smiling.

Look, White continued, *a Negro family moving in will start protests, we will be in the newspapers, there will be scenes,* trying to lighten the mood he quipped, *certainly not as, as, ugly as the ones in Little Rock... but there will be ugly scenes, pitting neighbor against neighbor, we must prevent this.* He stuttered and wished he had not said what was coming, but it was too late, it just popped out, *We need to go one step at a time.* The very line my father used so often in these conversations, in these arguments.

My father guffawed, *pitting neighbor against neighbor, sounds like a recent cocktail party I attended. You all sound like your now in agreement with what I was saying the other night. Go slow or there will be trouble. But the deal is done, you have a Negro neighbor and we are moving out. This is now your problem to deal with. This is what you wanted, equality and this is what you got.*

If these bright people had slowed down and thought, they could have seen that it was not that easy to sell a house in that neighborhood to a Negro. That the deal would have to go through a bank and banks did not give loans to colored folks. You did not sell a house, to anyone, in a matter of hours, they were being swindled, but not by Professor Harold Hill for band uniforms and trombones, my father did not want money, he wanted their dignity, he wanted to humiliate them and point out how hypocritical they were. He wanted to destroy them.

Well, I am sure you will enjoy getting to know the Washington's and it will all work out and my father, grinning, got up to leave. The room broke into a mob, everyone was yelling at him:

You cannot do this...
We have lawyers you know...
You will be blackballed...
Wait and see...
Be reasonable...
This will not stand...
I will not have a Negro family with 5 kids living on my block, screamed Dory Stevens.

Their faces were flushed, they were standing, yelling and gesticulating, all the venom was directed at my father, this refined group of people, so well-educated, had lost control.

My father, standing, facing the mob, slammed down his drink. He was intimidating, both in his expression and stature, only 5'8 but built like a fireplug and had played college football at Auburn University, he liked a fist-fight and according to him, never lost one. He was not to be challenged. He laughed, glared at them and as he moved away from the front door, back into the room, moved towards his neighbors, they stepped back, trying to regain composure, in fear of him. He stopped pointed at them and said *hypocrites, I did not sell the house to that family or any family, I just wanted to prove to you what fools you liberals are, what hypocrites you are. When push comes to shove you are weak and you say one thing but live a different way, look at you. Pitiful, you so easily ridiculed the folks in Little Rock in September, you are no different. You just think you are better.*

He turned, they stood stunned, too stunned to talk and out he went, leaving the door wide open behind him. He walked across the street, up the two flights of stairs, to the porch and entered the house sweating and pumping his fist in the air. He went to the dining room, opened the bar and poured a stiff drink and for the only time I remember he howled a like a wolf, then slammed it. Poured a second, added ice and coke and proceeded to describe his victory to his family. We sat on the couch and he roamed back and forth in front of us lecturing, doing a comedy routine, and venting. I was too frightened to move.

Someone shut the Stevens' front door and we can only imagine the damage that had been done. No opinions were changed, these good folks had been humiliated and dirtied but they continued down the correct road of history and like all people were brave but flawed. It would not be till after my father's lung operation and his inability to make it up the stairs that the for-sale sign went back into the yard and we moved. Prior to that the Whites moved to Pakistan and the cocktail parties ended or at least were kept quiet and we were not invited.

What happened to the Washingtons? If that was even their names. How did they feel about the whole affair? Humiliated or proud, indifferent toward crazy white folks. How did they tell the story? No one knows, except for perhaps my one lung father.

After the affair, my father had a repeating nightmare, he told no one about it, but sometimes we know things through other sensations. He dreamed he was a drunk Professor Harold Hill, stumbling and falling and trying to lead our neighbors, dressed in band uniforms, playing broken trombones and marching out of step and in various directions. In the sky was a colored children's choir, singing You Got to be Taught, (Carefully Taught). He always woke up singing the song himself, having it go around and around in his exhausted, hung-over brain.

You've got to be taught (carefully taught)
To hate and fear,
You've got to be taught
From year to year,
It's got to be drummed
In your dear little ear
You've got to be carefully taught.
You've got to be taught to be afraid
Of people whose eyes are oddly made,

And people whose skin is a diff'rent shade,
You've got to be carefully taught.
You've got to be taught before it's too late,
Before you are six or seven or eight,
To hate all the people your relatives hate,
You've got to be carefully taught!

Kennedy

You may wonder where was I on November 22, 1963, the day Jack Kennedy was assassinated down in Dallas. Where I was that afternoon needs to be preceded and understood by this story... a true story. It starts with my grandfather, Hugh D. Merrill, a former state of Alabama judge and Lieutenant Governor. See, the south, the solid south, had been democratic since the Civil War and the democratic party had two parts: the northern liberal side and the southern yellow dog democratic side, loyal to FDR's social and economic politics, but staunch segregationist. They were simply racists, fascists, the inventors and enforcers of Jim Crow. In 1959, Hugh D. Merrill, an influential member of the Democratic party fought hard and used his considerable power of persuasion to help get this liberal or liberal-ish northern Catholic democrat elected. It would be the last time that Alabama voted democratic. Jack Kennedy wrote Big Daddy Hugh, as I called him as a child, thanking him for helping him carry the state and get elected.

When it came time for the inauguration in January, it began to snow and it snowed a snow unlike anything anyone could remember in the Washington area. It was a blizzard, 18 inches. The roads were closed, no one could move, everyone was stuck in place, but the inauguration had to go on, so all the trucks, plows and workers moved snow off the parade route down Pennsylvania Ave and tried to dig out the outside grandstands for the audience. The few who showed up would see and hear the famous, "*ask not what your country can do for you*" speech.

As a 12-year-old, I cared nothing for the inauguration. I was at a friend's house, we were all going to spend the night and play tackle football in the snow. I begged, as only a 12-year-old middle-class child can beg, and pouted to get my way, but my parents came, picked me up and took me home so I could go to the inauguration the next morning. I was one sad pre-teen.

My mother worked for Senator John Sparkman of Alabama. When you see the parade with Kennedy in an open top car, a bad idea for the temp was about 18 degrees, but he and John Sparkman are laughing and waving at the almost non-existent parade crowd that had come to cheer, drink and celebrate his election. My father was at the top rung of the Agriculture Department, just below Presidential appointments. An appointment he hoped would be forth coming in the next several months, an appointment that never showed up. My mother worked for Senator John Sparkman, as his receptionist and perhaps more. My parents moved in the upper echelons of the Democratic party and were delegates to the 1956 convention. We used to go out to Robert Kennedy's home in McClain for political events and they seemed to know, and have a story about, everyone. Through these connections, they had been invited to the inauguration and the parties that evening and so we went, one of the few families who braved the cold and snow to sit on snow covered wooded benches. If the weather had been decent, like even 30 degrees and no snow, we would have had great seats, easy to see the speakers and watch the transfer of power from the Eisenhower administration to the New Frontier. In the freezing temperature and snow, though, there were no good seats.

I sat jiggling in the cold several yards down on the empty benches trying to keep my feet alive, keeping them warm had ended a half hour past. I imagined myself climbing Mt. Everest and played in my frozen mental fantasy, in time my mother grabbed my arm and through her whiskey-cigarette breath, she told me that the tiny old white haired man on the podium was Robert Frost, which meant nothing to me. As I returned from the side of my imaginary mountain climbing adventure I watched as he leaned into the storm, rasping into the microphone, a poet's voice lost in the wind and the wind rose and his poem written for the event lifted with his voice into the frozen air and the white pages containing the poem lifted into the whipping, cold wind.

I watched this old man with his gnarled hand, grabbing at the wind, trying to catch the fleeing poem but it was gone and some underling from the podium lead the brilliant poet away to the safety and warmth of the capital.

There was a huddle of men on the podium, this was the new President, Jack Kennedy, taking the oath of office, time passed, a smattering of applause and cheers, then the speech. Again, his words were blown into the wind. Yet these words I could hear. This brilliant young President, convinced that we were better as a united force than a smattering of individuals. We were more than individuals alone fighting for a piece of the American pie. He called out, exclaimed for a vision of unity, "*ask not what your country can do for you but what you can do for your country*". It was true and electric, there for a moment was only Jack Kennedy speaking: the snow and the cold were gone. He saw a unified and free nation of individuals striving for a greater goal. It was riveting and life changing for a young boy of 12.

So, on November 22, 1963 in Dallas, a bullet ripped his neck and the next exploded his skull, his death started the long march of time towards the trickle down, piss on the poor and middle class of Reagan and today's fascism of Trump. So, I was in 8th grade when it happened, in a mobile home styled classroom when the news came down, around 1:00 in the afternoon we learned that Kennedy was dead.

Rocketman

Wernher von Braun made the rockets, the terror weapons for Hitler that smashed indiscriminately into London killing thousands, scaring millions. He surrendered to the US at the end of the war and, with other scientists, came to work here for the United States. Kennedy was interested in going to the moon *not because it was easy but because it was hard*, as he said. So, the Nazi criminal got a pass, no jail, no trial and as far as I know, gave no apology. He ended up in Huntsville, Alabama and designed the firestone rockets that put the American satellites, then astronauts in space. Eventually his Saturn V rocket would send men to the moon. Kennedy had his head blown off in Dallas and did not live to see men bounce around on the lunar surface.

My family's connection to Alabama would lead to an invitation to meet with the famed German/American scientist and my parents dragged me along. They enjoyed introducing me to famous people, I was good looking for the most part, quiet and well-mannered. I think it was less for me than for them, like showing off some prized show pony to exhibit our family-ness.

We went into an empty conference room in a hotel in downtown Washington. I sat on a leather couch and then the Senator and the scientist entered. My Father and Mother got up to meet the scientist, they all shook hands and talked, I was distracted and paid no attention, just looked like the perfect son in my suit and well-shined shoes. I was at last introduced to Wernher von Braun and he shook my hand and patted me on the head, sat in a chair and he pulled me onto his knee. I stood leaning and half-sitting against him. The adults talked and smoked, I got away and stood behind a large table on the far side of the room.

I was excited to have meant the "American" who had invented the rockets I had seen on TV shooting astronauts into space. I had no other knowledge of his true history. I was lost in my own world when a photographer came in and the adults got up and a picture was taken of Sparkman, Father, Mother and the Nazi. WVB was smiling intensely at my mother, my father was completely self-aware and stared directly into the camera, showing his bright white false teeth to the photographer. Sparkman, eyes half-closed, seemed asleep but happy like a cartoon drunk. I was now only one degree of separation from Adolf Hitler. WVB was the man that Hitler had counted on to win the war, but it had already slipped down the toilet of history for the Germans. Hitler thought it could still be won by some stroke of magic: science, physics and rockets.

Now I look back and think of perhaps Hitler and WVB's last meeting, with Hitler grasping Wernher's hand in both of his, saying, *you will rain rockets down on London and we shall win; we, the German people, will yet be victorious and you can do this for me.* WVB, returning the warm handshake saying *yes, Mein Fuhrer, we will do this, I will do this for you,* the old *Heil Hitler* and then they parted. The hand that had often shaken Hitler's had shaken mine and patted me on the head.

The School for the Sexual Education for Young Girls and Boys

In Alexandria, Virginia in the 1960's there were no high school sports for girls, it was not deemed lady-like. Sports in this southern city outside Washington, DC were for boys, except for cheerleading, tennis, swimming and golf. Girls' sports were of little significance in the process of educating girls. Unlike the Hot Shed.

We often played in the shed. It should have been officially named The School for the Sexual Education for Young Girls and Boys. The shed sat in an empty lot waiting to have a home built on it. It was the last empty lot in the neighborhood, sitting at the end of Fountain Street and the entrance to St. Agnes private girls' school. With its brick entrance gates, facing the shed, on which was engraved *St Agnes School for the Education of Young Women*.

Cindy was a classmate, had been one since my second round of third grade. I had flunked. She was best friends with Richard's little sister Lauren Brooks, we were 13 and the girls were 11. We knew about sex but not much, mostly from the bragging of the 16-year-old boys on the block. They would disappear into Martha's house, go to the basement and not come out to play street ball for hours. Then, when they did, the stories of their exploits would fly. They would have gotten Martha's bra and blouse off or open, rubbed their hands on the outside of her undies, we did not use the term panties and underwear was not very sexy back then just functional and white.

Cindy would spend the night at Lauren and Richard's house and I would stay over also. I would make-out with Cindy while we were supposed to be watching TV in the basement. About every 15 minutes, the girls would laugh and run upstairs to Lauren's room and come down later and the silly fun would all start again. Nothing was guaranteed. One evening Cindy would let me open her blouse, another she let me pull up her bra but not French Kiss her. The next time we would kiss the French way, but she would not let me touch her small breasts. The mystery went unsolved.

School was out and none of us went to camp or had parents around during the day. The long summer day was open, we would ride our bikes to the school ground where the Parks Department paid older high school kids to open up a large wooden green box with a padlock. In the box were arts and crafts, balls of every description, jump ropes and other goodies. We would sit for good part of the day on the school swings, at times swinging double, standing up and flying. Boy and girl, face to face, bodies touching in a vertical missionary position, standing and flying back and forth through the hot Virginia southern humid air. Lips inches from each other, cheeks touching, the girl's hair flying into my face, bodies touching, breast to breast, crotch to crotch, intimate and the closest we came to sex. Swinging was better and more fun than making out. Hand on top of hand it was as erotic an experience anyone might ever have.

Just prior to parents getting home on the bus or in their cars, we would ride back to the block and throw the bikes down and run into the small unlocked plywood shed. The room with a single window, just a square opening cut into the plywood and covered with a hinged shutter. We all loved the smell of the darkroom the smell of hot wood and glue. The shed was empty, had been built but had not yet been used to house construction materials. We would step into the hot darkness, open the shuttered window to let in hot air, but that hot air was cooler than the trapped air in the room. We were all physically hot and sweaty from our bike ride but the perspiration now came pouring off our young bodies in the super-heated shed. There were three couples, me and Cindy, Tom and Diane, and Richard and Lauren who were brother and sister and kept watch and sometimes even kissed. Richard would try to get Lauren to show her small tits to us all. Tom and Diane, Cindy and me would lie on the floor, roll on top of each other: wrestle, kiss, touch, and laugh. Our play was not an attempt to actually make love or to score or get laid. It was play, simply making out, of kind of making out and exploring.

Sometimes the older boys and Martha came and ran us off, except for Cindy, Diane and Lauren, of course. They stayed while Richard, Tom and myself sulked in a tree fort at the edge of the woods, watching. They left the shed, lighting cigarettes and the girls ran off towards Martha's house holding hands, waving at us sitting on limbs of the oak tree and laughing.

The girls went to Martha's house to tell themselves they were grown-up, that being held down was fun, that not taking no for an answer was part of the game, it was the way things were and anyway the older boys liked them. They did not believe the lies they told each other and the lump of fear, doubt, regret and humiliation in their throats would hang around for a life time. Repetition reinforces the rules and the responses.

This was one of the first times, but not the last, they would learn what boys, teens and men thought their bodies were for. They learned that their voices were only for making sounds, not giving commands, there exasperated *no's* were not orders, but flexible guidelines or merely suggestions. Cindy told Lauren as Richard and I spied on them, having crawled on our bellies into the door way of his sister's room:

I haven't had sex, never would do that even with the Jake (one of the older boys). *We did more than make-out and frenching, though.*

Lauren giggled and said *tell me about one hundred times in less than 10 seconds.*

He puts his finger inside me, just a little at first not much and I melted and for a little while I could not fight back. I just lay there, and his fingers were touching me here and then he touches me here then all over and kisses me here.

Lauren repeats another 100 times on *no really, reallyreallyreally...*

We could not see where Cindy pointed, only imagine, and

dream in vagueness. There was a long pause, then Lauren mused, a kind of talking and thinking at the same moment, not sure what was going to come out, not sure what her thoughts were even to herself, she spoke searchingly, *no one has ever done that to me, not yet, not with their finger, I do not think that will happen till I go steady.*

Cindy, Richard and I all thought the same: *of course no one has felt you up or touched you there, you do not have a boyfriend and the older boys let her hang around, but have not bothered to even try and kiss her.*

Cindy did not say what we were all thinking, that would have been mean. Instead she said, *I do not want to ever go steady, you know you cannot even talk to another guy when you are going steady. I do not think I could manage that no way, I love guys.*

Lauren and she laughed and began to wrestle, they giggled and rolled over on the bed and saw us on our hand and knees listening from the door. We ran, and they took off after us. We raced down the stairs, into the yard and down the street, heading unknowingly the two blocks from our School for the Education of Young Women and Men to the entrance of Saint Agnes School for the Education of Young Women.

Penny Parking

It is only two 16-year old kids, fucking around in the backseat of a red Impala. A 1968 red Impala convertible with congressional license plates, air conditioning, big front seats and big backseats, AM radio, a playground for high school exploits, tales or just good old lies.

The steam rises from the back seat of the car and the windows are slightly fogged. With Penny's legs akimbo, parked near the construction zone of the new Catholic elementary school, the cop car pulled up right behind them and he got out of the car. He looked through the window, watching the humping, sweating, groping, moaning teenagers, for no one knows how long. Eventually, they saw the policeman and he tapped on the window as if he had just walked up and glanced in. He had gotten an eyeful. He took Penny as she was, naked and barefoot and put her in his cop car, came back and got her shoes, socks, skirt and blouse. The officer climbed into his cop car, pretending to do some paper work on a clip board.

I sat in the driver's seat of the red Impala... waiting. Penny covering up as best she could, bending forward and covering her torso with her crossed, hugging arms. He spoke to her and she was crying and begging not to have her parents find out.

The cop came back to the Impala and got Penny's bra and panties. He checked them out, carefully folded them and took them back to the cop car and got in the passenger seat. He placed them on top of the rest of her clothes, Penny sat naked. I watched from the backseat of the Impala having climbed over the seat, crouched down and peering out the rear window. He finally handed her the bra.

She just sat there listening to him and seemed to have relaxed a bit and was not crying so hard. She put on the bra first, red-faced, humiliated and looking constantly at him as she slid the bra around her waist, the cups behind her back and straps off. She fastened the bra snaps and rotated the bra around her torso. I watched fascinated, as did the police officer. She slid her arms through the shoulder straps, in a single perfected movement pulled herself up and the bra covered her breasts.

She seemed to smile at something the officer said, and they seemed to be having a conversation; she had stopped crying. He must have assured her he was not going to take her to jail and tell her parents. I was sure, but never found out what was said, it was just a good guess. It did not occur to me that he might have been complimenting her or setting up a time for sexual favors. Back then, as a child, a teen, I saw grown-ups as good people, especially teachers, policemen and so on. Well, like many, I was a fool. I figured he was giving her a lesson on God and being good.

She was still sitting with her bra on and nothing else and now laughing. Her head disappeared behind the seat and the silhouette of the cop, then she half stood in the back seat wiggling about. She was putting on her skirt, and then he handed her the panties and she proceeded to do the same gesture and put them on, then socks and then her loafers. At last he took the shirt and handed it to her. She put it on, buttoned up the blouse leaving the top two buttons unbuttoned, showing a bit of her cleavage.

They talked a bit more, they got out of the car, and came back to the Impala. I had by now climbed back into the driver's seat. He opened the passenger door for her, she got in, he shut it and came around to the driver's side. The window was down, and I was looking at my feet, completely intimidated by the police officer. I waited.

Penny sat next to me in the passenger's seat, leaning away from me and towards the passenger's door, adjusting her clothes. The cop told me he was not going to take us "in" because my dad was a member of Congress, he could tell that from the congressional license plate. Next time things might not go as well. He gave more advice about girls and sex, about not letting my father down. I knew my father was not a congressman.

He asked which state he was from and I simply lied, kind of, and said *Alabama*. He smiled and went back to his car. He motioned for us to leave and he followed us to the intersection at Seminary Road. I turned left, and he waited, as if deciding which way to go and turned right toward the seminary.

Penny would get pregnant the next year, a junior in high school, screwed by Fred, they would have a child. Penny's older sister had gotten pregnant but was less lucky, was far less lucky.

Penny Story: second act

Her old man worked construction and drove a 1961 Ford pickup. He drove his three-month-along pregnant daughter to the doctor's at Haskell's Mansion on Seminary Road. The illegal abortion would be performed on an early Saturday morning when Kelli was supposed to at the school for an overnight, some sort of practice, and would not be home till Sunday evening. By then, she would complain of a stomach ache, stay home on Monday and Tuesday if need be, but no one else would ever know.

We know that she was not a virgin, had been pregnant, and had had the fearful abortion. A few days, a few hours, a simple operation and the past would not intrude on a bright and perfect future. The clinic was in the doctor's house, the visit was scheduled for early and was never recorded in the Doctor's appointment book, like the other regular appointments always were. The Doctor was one of the few brave men trying to prevent the medical disasters for women who sought out illegal back-alley abortions. He had seen the septic ward at the Alexandria General Hospital with young, middle-aged and even older women, who for a variety of reasons, had gotten coat hanger abortions.

Women who, in the back rooms of empty store fronts, paid $300 to spread their legs, lie on a metal industrial table and have a catheter and needle shoved up their vagina to pierce the lining of the cervix, try to scrape away the tissue, end the pregnancy. Here, under a light bulb, they trusted greater powers of hope or God to prevent them from getting infections or complications, perhaps uterine perforation; there were many, take your choice. These places had no general anesthesia or pain killers, just sheer determination and fear of having another or a first child drove them. Rape, incest, date rape, a little cheating, perhaps with a man from the wrong race, the demands of a boss or father or not knowing who the father was: the reasons were not trivial.

You do not face death and sickness and the loss of a pregnancy as a method of birth control or due to a lack of character.

They usually returned home, fought the pain of cramps, heavy bleeding weakening their resolve, until the pain and the loss of blood could no longer be ignored and off to the hospital and the septic ward they went.

Haskle performed abortions, but only for the daughters of the well-to-do, those in his *class*, there were not many and they all had gone well. How a truck and tractor driver on a construction crew got his daughter into Haskle's hidden clinic is unknown, but Haskle must have known Kelli and her dad. Every abortion was a risk, and this was outside his comfort zone, outside his class and beyond what he said he would do. How Jake Smoot even knew Dr. Haskle was never known discovered or figured out, but Jake got his daughter in for the procedure. All started well, a mild anesthetic, tubes pushed in to widen the cervix and the insertion of the curette. Haskle scraped the uterus, removed the lining carefully, checked to make sure all of the needed tissue had been removed and that there was little chance of infection. Then Kelli began to bleed and her father looked on in terror as the blood soaked through one pad after another. Haskle applied pressure, began to panic himself as it was clear this was not normal, and that he could not take her to the hospital, but had to stop the bleeding here in the basement of his large and palatial home.

Kelli turned whiter than pale, then an odd bluish gray as she stopped breathing and the oxygen was no longer in her blood. Jake and Dr. Haskle watched her life slip away. She died that Saturday morning on the table in Dr. Haskle's basement lab. Nothing could be done to save her, the hospital was not a choice, both understood this reality of jail and disgrace. Kelli died at 11:03, but did not stop bleeding.

Penny was almost forgotten in all the horror of the day, but she had come with Kelli, they were close as if one and it was Penny that Kelli had told about her sexual experiences and then turned up pregnant. Jake had smartly chosen to take Penny along, it would teach her a thing or two and help in the conspiracy to make sure that their mom, his wife, never found out. Now the conspiracy took on a deeper and more powerful union, a death was involved, the death of a vital, bright and deeply loved daughter and sister.

Haskle devised the plan to make the legal ramifications go away, he took care of the body, but we do not know how. Jake and Penny simply told the story that Kelli had run off with a boy and would be back, a lie Kelli's mother believed and thought it was about sowing wild oats but the only flowers here would not exist above Kelli's non-existent grave. She was a statistic, a lost teen in the *On the Road* generation of the 1960's, just a runaway in the world of hippies, yippies and druggies. Never a lost runaway to Penny and Jake, but God help her mother, who never found out the truth.

I think Penny would have done anything to not re-break her father's heart, but we all are sexual beings, driven by forces beyond our own control a good part of the time. Penny is, was and always will be a good and wonderful person. God bless and you all pray for Kelli and the rest.

FW 18

A decade back the term FW 18 caught my eye as I looked at the personals on the back page of the local weekly tabloid. I sat sipping coffee at Broadway Café and I laughed at the term, then I realized that FW 18 meant female, white and 18. The first thing that popped into my mind had a different meaning, it was a different story.

I saw FW 18 in the personals section. It was amusing that people advertised themselves for sexual play, men and women, moms and grand dads, all in the local weekly newspaper, shopping for each other, for someone, anyone. Today I guess it has all moved on-line presenting a fantasy of possibilities for the lonely and bored. It is dope, or better, dopamine pleasure. A pleasure that, for a moment, puts aside fears and anxiety. Affording the pleasure of searching for another while being safe, anonymous and alone. But FW 18, that day, called forward other memories, it meant something different—to me.

You're Free, white and 18 so get out. It was what my father told me on my 18th birthday. April 28, 1968, kind of a gift for my high school graduation, perhaps a birthday present as well? This boy was not sure. In fact, I was not even living under the same roof as him.

By then, my mother and father were just recently divorced. My mother dressed for my graduation and went to the school after a couple of strong drinks, as was her habit.

I barely got out of high school. It was never guaranteed that with my inabilities and grades, with skipping school and making art, that I actually would graduate but I did and she was relieved. My father, living in some Arlington apartments 20 miles from the school, started to get ready for the graduation but fell over drunk and when he finally headed off for the school auditorium; he took a wrong turn and ended up in some bar, never showed up. He was not missed.

I had started to go to graduation, got dressed, put on a tie and school pants, not jeans. I was forcing myself, I was going to do this because I was supposed to, out of guilt, because my mother was going. I was not going because I needed or wanted to. I was already gone from high school, from that culture that had supported and put up with me, helped me survive from 14 to 18. But in my heart and head, I was already in the ghetto in Baltimore, where I already had an apartment. All that high school meant for me was past, a memory before I had even gotten out the school door. I was the ghost going to a celebration of others' futures.

I pulled into the parking lot with the black robe in the backseat. I sat looking at the back entrance of the school, parked and went in. Only my Mother saw my non-graduation and I cannot imagine her embarrassment and sadness, but nothing was ever said. There was no dinner or event planned for afterwards. She knew I would not be home till very late, after 1:00 AM. This was normal family behavior.

It was good that the family had fallen apart and only my mother had attended because, in fact, to go anywhere with them was a disaster. Growing up, I had learned to avoid any social events or even private contact with my parents, I had learned distance, to stay away. Every public interaction became a blow to self-respect. A calamity, a fiasco, a catastrophe, an embarrassment leading to nightmares of silent rage. "Hugh" learned his lessons well. *Keep clear.* Even getting ice cream with my drunken father would turn into a frightening experience with him yelling at some family, scaring children and a fist fight.

I sat sipping a cold beer in the car overlooking the Potomac River at Roaches Run, with airplanes from the National Airport taking off, flying just overhead on Friday night, the evening prior to graduation. I swore that never again would my parents have the chance to screw up my life. A plane flew over, roaring engines and blinking lights, I looked up remembering a high school football game, playing quarterback and calling the signals, when I glanced at a disturbance in the stands, two men were in a fight. Of course it was my father, beating another man and the cops running up the bleachers to drag him off to jail.

Hut 1 hut 2, the ball was hiked, I simply put my head down and charged forward. Yardage gained, not bad. The amazed coach was yelling encouragement thinking that I had seen something and changed the play. Like much of the good in my life, it was by happenstance and luck that success showed up. And it did show up.

I took my graduation robe up to the music room where we were to change and the door was locked. It was just off the side door into the auditorium and I could hear the festivities and the speaker's muffled voice down the hall. I hung my robe on the doorknob and started down the hall to view the ceremony from the balcony but changed my steps and went back through the school toward the parking lot and my beat-up Corvair, missing the passenger's seat.

Earl stepped out of the custodian closet, we smiled, I loved his smell, a smell of pipe tobacco, and sweeping compound. We sat on the 10-gallon drums of cleaner he had just dragged from the closet.

You not going.

No can't, just does not seem right somehow.

Saw my son graduate from Parker Gray, last year, wore, my Sunday best and the family had quite a sing-song for him.

No party for me, think my mom is watching in there.

What about your daddy?

He is at the bottom of a bottle by this time of day, we both laughed.

I know that mmmmm m seen that mmmmm m.

I stood to leave and Earl got up took my hand and, with

genuine warmth, looked me in the eye, grinned and held my hand warmly for just a moment. Just held my hand, then we laughed. It would be the last time I stepped into this school.

"You going to knock out everything, but quit-it" he smiled and said, "*everything*. But quit-it."

I laughed, for again I had been given advice that I did not understand and knew better than to ask for an explanation. Knowing can take time, I got in the car and headed back to Roaches Run to watch folks "graduate" into the sky, journey just over-head on their trips to future.

Dying

How many times he should have died is unknown, but there were many times he was on the verge of dying and somehow kept on going. When I went to see him in the veteran's hospital outside of DC he was as thin as a rail, his skin hung on him and he was, of course, green with bright yellow eyes, not the nice yellow but the slime pus yellow with a bit of dayglow marker mixed in, jaundice, liver damage, a one lung smoker, and a tobacco addict from the time he was 10 or 12 years old, the filter-less kind for the first three decades of his life.

He drank about a fifth of whiskey a day and this went on for decades. He would quit now and then, only to return to the bottle with full confidence and a love for a drink that only a southern brought up on the bottle can know. It was, as far as I could see, his one true love.

He had risen to the top, went as far as you could go in the Agriculture Department and the civil service. He had hoped to be appointed Undersecretary of Agriculture by John Kennedy but it did not occur and so the drinking increased and he went down the chute. He went down quickly and fell hard and there would be no rebounding from this tumble. His drunkenness and bad temper took away his charm, his looks, his ability to be funny and clever, his ability to remember who when what where why and how. Everything in his drunken state of mind was an insult and a fight and he got in many. He had lost all control of his manners and behavior.

Drinking started at 4:00 in the morning, leading to a day of passing out and reviving. It had done him in professionally, physically and as a person. Once this man walked with the powerful, congressmen, senators, scientists and even presidents. He was now a bum, but a bum with a steady income and great health care. His fall to the bottom came quickly, from near Undersecretary of Agriculture to a security guard and then attendant at a dry cleaner. He could hold down no job for more than a week, not even the most menial job. Drinking was what he could do, and he was great at it. Again and again, he crawled up only to hit bottom. Crawl up a notch and stumble drunken into the bottom of some stinking muck-filled hole. Only to bounce up and career off in some new direction. The gravity of alcoholism is strong and no matter what program he got sober with, it always turned out the same, back like a stone thrown from the bridge over Owl Creek, he sank to the bottom and never broke the rope and never rose to the surface. He hung out with the bottom feeders, no desire to see the light again.

He is the only person I have heard of that was thrown out of Alcoholics Anonymous. He was good at whatever he put his mind to but success was short termed and disrupted by his base nature, his love of sex, drinks, recognition, and gambling. So, again when he hit the bottom and was for the moment saved by AA he became an ardent follower of the twelve step Alcoholics Anonymous program. With his remaining charm, wit, cleverness and his ability to lie he rose quickly to a leadership position. He helped others in their hour of need, guided them through the tough nights, helping them stay sober and soon was in charge of the group meeting at the high school I had attended across the street my mother's garden apartment.

I came home from the Maryland Institute of Art on a Wednesday evening to find the ground floor patio apartment blazing with light and drunken songs. My father had convinced the Alcoholic Anonymous group to come over from the school to the ground floor apartment for a drink. A drink just to prove to themselves that they were no longer addicted and could take alcohol or leave it.

This, of course, went against everything taught, everything they had learned, but it does not take much to tip the scale in favor of tipping the wrist and having just one drink. One led to many and soon the ex-World War II vets, as most of the men and women in the group were, were drunk as skunks singing *buffalo girl won't you come out tonight*. It was a sad, funny and all around miserable scene, shirt tails out, staggering middle aged drunken men and women singing and stumbling as they danced. Some passed out, half in a chair and half slid down to the floor as if their bones had turned to Jell-O. The air filled with tobacco smoke, some people were pushing a woman back into my bedroom. Some man had fallen out the apartment door and blocked the door to the laundry. A neighbor was now separated from her wet laundry by a man dead to the world for the time being. I left without a word, the police came and somehow the party ended without arrests and the drunks slept in their cars till they could drive home. I did not return for several months, by then, my father was long gone having run off with some 19-year-old girl to live in Florida. Continuing to go from barroom society to sobriety to drunkenness and back to the hospital and from the hospital to rehab. Back to sober living only to go way off the wagon and then return to the hospital always tinged green skin and deadly yellow eyes and often very near death.

We would get the calls from Florida and some administrator in a hospital would inform us that *Mr. James W. Merrill SR. was near death and did we want to come down.* We had no interest in doing that and he never died after one of these calls but instead he bounced back from comas and liver disease, returning to life from glowing yellow greenness and screaming mindlessly. He often attacked the poor nurses who tried to tend to him, grabbing their breasts, showing them his shriveled manhood. He would be dead to the world then coming alive for a few moments of terror for the staff and perhaps for himself. Then, thankfully, dropping off into a narcotic induced stupor. Only to rise again like a wicked ghost in a poorly written Shakespeare play. But he refused to give in and die.

It would be another decade before he would die. He did well in that last decade, opening Jim and Mary Merrill's Greeting Service. He had a scam where he was paid by merchants in his retirement community to go and meet new comers, new home owners and bring them a gift basket from local merchants so as to entice them to shop in Spring Hill and not go to the nearby malls with their super stores. He kept taking baskets to the same people in his neighborhood and claiming them all as new comers, they liked the scam. They got lots of free stuff and

Jim and Mary got paid. Not only did they get paid but they got points from a company in Norton, Iowa that made pens and other stuff with a business' name on it. Pens, caps, tee shirts, scarfs, lanyards, ashtrays, you name it they could put your name on it. They also produced all sorts of novelties for house and home. My father used his points wisely and his place was filled with the commercially unusual.

I got the call in the middle of the night that he had died. It came from my sister and I told her I was not going to attend his funeral, saw no reason to, but she paid for the ticket and so I flew down separate from her. My brother, Jimbo, came up from Maryland. This would be the last time the three of us were together. We stayed at my mother's home in Tampa. She did not feel it was wise to go to the funeral and I really think she had no heart for it at all and with good reasons.

My sister Jane and Jimbo and I drove out to the Spring Hill retirement community. We knew no one there and it was the first time I had met his new wife, Mary. At the funeral home, I refused to go in and view the body, that was for my brother and sister. Most of the memories I had of the man were ugly or distressing. I felt I did not need to see him dead in his coffin and hear some minister who knew nothing about him say what a great man he had been, a vet and read his resume, all a pack of distortions and lies.

At 5 years old I had seen him almost dead in the National Institute of Health in DC. He was one of the first men to have a lung removed, a very experimental operation, they quartered him, removed the lower lobe of one of his lungs, ran tubes out of his nose, mouth, his stomach and his side. The tubes all connected to pumps with blinking lights, he should have died then and this should have been my last memory of him but he was tough and hung in there. He survived and returned to smoking as if he had an extra lung implant rather than part of one removed. This was in the 50's and he would live for decades whoring, smoking and drinking, entering rehab and hospitals when his liver gave out and each time he'd bounce back, a little worse, but still kicking.

There were the images of him in my memory, glowing, day glow green with hepatitis in the veteran's hospital, screaming and falling over drunk in Baskin-Robbins ice cream, of sending everyone's dinners back at Blackie's Steak House, even people he did not know and who were not sitting at our table. We were, of course, asked to leave.

Several years later, I remember him drunk in the back of a police car when he had beaten a policeman half to death and broken his arm. There he was: evil eyed, screaming and peering out of the car handcuffed. Or the time I looked up from the high school football field and over in the stands I see a fight and yes, it is my father beating the crap out of some guy. Turns out it was over a bet on the game.

These images go on, his fights with my brother, beating up a black man in front of Mike's liquor store in DC for god knows what reason. I wanted nothing more to do with him so I stayed out of the chapel and when they brought the casket out and put it in the hearse I joined my brother and sister in the limo, but I smartly did not have to look on his dead face. All the seniors citizens in the chapel and there were many, because everyone in an old folks community loves a funeral. It will be the major subject for discussion at parties and BBQs until the next one and in the old age community they come quickly, one and the next. Everyone who can attends these affairs. It does not matter if you know the stiff, everyone is invited and everyone plays their sympathetic part well.

So, the folks filed out and got into their cars, they knew the routine and we did not. I expected to drive for several miles to some cemetery, but this was much shorter, in fact, it was very short, the hearse pulled out, drove to the far end of the parking lot and pulled off on a gravel road into the cemetery. It was less than a 100 yards away. All the cars followed, the black hearse and the black limo we were riding in, all drove about 100 yards and stopped.

The long line of cars with their headlights on had lined up as best they could behind the hearse and limo and drove their part of the 100 yard funeral parade. The procession never made it out of the parking lot. They stopped left their vehicles and got out and walked the short distance to the grave site. I stood their amazed at having viewed the worlds shortest funeral procession in history. But traditions matter, especially to those near their own end of being. The minister and the funeral staff were busy opening the hearse and putting the casket on a rolling cart to move it to the open grave, just down the hill perhaps another 30 yards away. The fresh dirt lay covered by a green tarp next to the grave and away rolled my father, his final moments above ground had come.

I turned back, standing next to the limo and saw every car was still in the parking lot, cars with their lights on, and engines running to cool them down, sparkling large American cars in the bright Florida sunshine. Everyone had piled out and walked respectfully up the road and into the cemetery, down the grass hill to the grave. My brother and sister also headed down for the final prayer, I lingered at the car leaning on the hearse and watched.

A car drove up slowly from an adjacent road in the grave yard and stopped at a rather large tomb stone. Out came three older women, I thought they were going to walk down to my father's funeral, figured they were late arrivals from out of the community but one woman looking very, very, sad could not go any further. She stopped, put her hand on the larger tomb stone and started to cry, really cry. It struck me that my father had done something good, he had helped her, done something good for here.

He had helped many people he did not really know. It was his family and those that were close to him that he damaged and terrorized. I saw that down the hill the coffin was going in the ground and was interrupted by one of the women asking me if there was a way out of the cemetery since the road was blocked by the cars from my father's funeral procession.

The women who had been crying was getting back in her car, I ask if they had come to my father's funeral? No, she said they came every weekend to visit the fallen hero's memorial. Her son had been killed in the Vietnam War and his body had not returned. I, for the first time all day, felt a true sadness, I felt deep compassion at her loss and the foolishness of that war. All I cared about was helping her get out of the graveyard and around my father's stalled funeral procession. I guided them through an area of grass, where they could by pass our hearse and the rest of the cars in the procession. I think they thought I worked for the funeral home. So I helped guide them past the line of cars and back onto the pavement of the parking lot, then, sadly watched as they drove out of the chapel grounds and turn left onto the street and drove off. I felt deep sorrow for her loss, her young son killed in a war of waste and murder.

I felt people moving by me and looked to see that the burial was complete, everyone was returning to their cars. We got in the limo and headed away, following the hearse on the road curving back onto the street in front of the funeral home. We then parked in front, got out, said nice things to the minister and director and headed back to Mary's and my late father's home.

I do not know if Mary had a reception later or a wake, perhaps they had a drunken wake. We stayed just long enough to have one beer and talk a bit. As we left, I needed to go to the bathroom and stood pissing into a toilet with a toilet seat and lid of clear plastic. Inside the seat and the lid were 100 dollar bills, they looked real but must have been fake, like so much of my life and certainly my father's. A fake thousand-dollar toilet seat with Norton Iowa Novelty Company clearly engraved in the Lucite on the rim of the toilet lid. He had bought it with points from the Jim and Mary Merrill Greeting Service. I washed my hands with free soap from the same company and dried my hand on Norton hand towels. We left.

As we drove, my brother described my father's hawk like face in the coffin, an image I had avoided and did not care to hear about. But the six pack of PBRs in the cooler we had so thoughtfully brought was making the afternoon lighter and deadly funny. Jimbo, by far the most abused by my father, thought "it was hysterically funny how tight and yellow his skin was across his skull. It was as if, if, all the fat had been sucked out from under the skin," he howled. My brother pronounced in joy and laughter "just a bag of skin and bones, yellow skin drawn tight over bones."

I had once seen my father scold my brother, Jimbo, for handing him a hammer, hammerhead first. "You never hand a man a hammer by that end, always by the handle don't you know anything, for Christ sakes." On he went belittling Jimbo, his son, a 12-year-old boy, a boy who was so, so, "stupid" that he did not know how to hand a hammer to another person. What a fool Jimbo must have felt like then and oh so often. That was the way things went. The Father was dead and buried and his sons had quickly knocked off the PBRs, in the first 25 miles of the drive back to Tampa.

Driving, I pulled over at a liquor store on Nebraska Avenue as we entered Tampa and bought a bottle of Jack and a 12 pack, opened the bottle and took a deep hit, opened another beer and chased the warm whiskey down my throat. Passed the bottle to my brother, as my sister does not drink and was not amused by any of my brother's dark humor, or our beginning a long night of drinking in the car on the journey home. She had loved her father and was in many ways his identical reflection.

She sat in the backseat of the car deeply pissed off. But then she had been deeply pissed off like him all of her life. The 50-mile ride home had become a cheap circus side-show, my brother and I drinking and making fun of the crap we had grown up with. My sister tried to point out all the good he had done but soon gave up trying and looked out the window counting the miles to freedom from her insensitive brothers.

The final miles passed quickly and at last everyone was quiet, at last in their own worlds as we pulled into the drive of the house on Nance Avenue. My brother went to the garage and pulled out the barbeque grill rolled it out on the driveway and started the charcoal. My sister opened the fridge and took out the chicken, covered in plastic wrap and soaking in Wishbone Italian dressing.

I had to piss and went into the ancient bathroom of my long-gone grandmother. Pulled down my zipper and slipped out my penis and aimed it at the porcelain toilet with a porcelain flush handle. The old bathroom was dim and cool and in the twilight, I looked at my reflection in the mirror and let out a stream of yellow piss. Grinned, as I thought of the Lucite toilet seat my father had "purchased" with Norton Novelty points. Most likely took his last crap on it before his liver finally gave out, lost his mind and memory and was hauled off to the hospital as a raving sack of bones. I looked down at the piss splashing into the toilet, finished, flushed and saw the spiral of water swirl around and around then go down the drain.

Post Script: Investing in Life?

All the money, all the property, the furniture, two or more inheritances, stocks and bonds and other riches were all pissed away. All gone by the day I left and caught the Greyhound to Baltimore to go to the Maryland Institute College of Art. I had $100 in my pocket saved from working construction the summer of 1968. I packed a seaman's bag full of clothes, some art supplies and my stuff. Pulled the cord tight and threw it over my shoulder and headed to the bus station in Washington DC. It did not occur to me to think about, or question where all the money had gone. That would come many decades later.

In my life of wealth and privilege we moved in a slow downward spiral but never got too low. Moving from owning homes, three houses that are now worth millions in Alexandria, Virginia, to renting. We first moved from our last house on Fountain Street to the 15th floor of a fancy apartment high rise, Southern Towers. When my father finally left for good, my mother and I moved to a smaller apartment on the 9th floor. From there, across the highway, less than a mile away to Seminary Forest a garden apartment complex, to a third floor two bedroom. The last move was to the ground floor of the same apartment complex and there my mother would stay till she retired to her mother's home in Hide Park in Tampa, Florida. We simply slipped downward but always were well off, always had a car, healthcare, a little extra money, food and clothes. I was never poor as a child.

Yet, a huge amount of money passed through my father's hands. Enough for several generations, enough to pay for college for my sister, brother and I, had that been a priority. We had a lot, more than enough, enough to make money make money and create wealth, but it was all pissed away. After my parent's divorce, we lived on my mother's salary from her job located in the New Senate Office Building, working for Senator John Sparkman, the guy in the car with Jack Kennedy at his inauguration, both in top hats. She worked for Sparkman for just over 20 years. It was a good salary (especially for a woman), but where had all the other money gone? There were no trust funds for kids, no college funds or saving accounts, and no stocks or bonds. Nothing left to inherit.

We had lived not like smart wealthy people, making money from their money, adding to wealth through smart investments. We lived rich, spending every dime and for the most part spending it on crap. From cars to monogrammed towels and bedspreads, all of it, all of that shit is in a landfill someplace. We bought property in Florida and Virginia, not for an investment, but to be "land owners". That property today is worth a fortune both in Northern Virginia and Central Florida, in fact some of it was right in the middle of Disney World. Property bought for dollars and sold at a loss. A lot of the money was gambled away, paid to lawyers to get my father off assault charges for beating up people even a couple of police officers, the money went to gallons of whiskey and of course rehab clinics. It went for women, rose bushes, cars suits. Mink stoles and chinchilla coats, hand painted toy soldiers from England, carpeting wall to wall and more, all gone, not a dime left as I headed to the Greyhound terminal.

I put down the $4.50 on the counter of the Greyhound ticket window and bought my one-way ticket. The sea-bag went into the cargo compartment and I took a window seat about half-way back on the bus. We shoved off and sped down the Baltimore-Washington Parkway to downtown Baltimore. I collected my bag, threw it over my shoulder and headed off to the Marlboro apartment building on Eutaw Avenue. There, I had a room with my brother, a faculty/graduate student at Maryland Institute College of Art and Bob Brown, a painter and drug addict.

The Marlboro was the once grad apartment building for the wealthy at the turn of the century. The Cone Sisters lived there, the ones who went to Paris often and collected paintings by Picasso, Matisse, Degas and others. Those paintings now make up the foundation of the Baltimore Museum of Art modern art collection. The building had all marble and brass fixtures, ornate wood and plaster ornamentation and beautiful hard wood floors. Its days of having carriages opened by well-dressed doormen were over. Once, getting an invitation to a Marlboro garden party meant that you had reached the heights of society in Maryland. Eutaw Avenue once glorious with magic Brownstone homes owned by doctors, lawyers and the best of society was now a ghetto's ghetto. All these old homes were cut up to make cheap apartments for the influx of Black folks escaping the South. Coming north to be treated with dignity, to get a good job and to become something. Instead they were overcharged, cheated, abused, robbed and raped at every opportunity.

This once grand-street and apartment building of seven stories was now inhabited by roaches, poor people, blacks, poets, filmmakers, actresses, artists of all descriptions. Ginsberg and Cage were in and out of town and stayed in the Marlboro and in Bolton Hill. Devine and John Waters lived in the building and Pink Flamingos would be made in the coming year. Yeah, I got to know them all and many more. But that would be later.

Today was my first day alone in the city, not yet a member of this amazing community. I had to walk from the bus station to Eutaw Place, to the Marlboro. I got my key, went in and set up my studio. I came out onto Howard Street, walked several blocks north and waited for the light to change to cross over and enter the Bolton Hill neighborhood. The light changed, and I stepped off the curb, my sea-bag on my shoulder and tripped and fell flat on my face in the street. People rushed by as I scrambled to recover, to pick up my sea-bag and scrape myself off the hot August pavement. I began again, the light changed, with my bag over my other shoulder I headed off, dodging traffic, horns honking and being flipped off. I ran past the angry drivers and swerving cars to the safety of the sidewalk. Hoping my head-first dive into the street had no deeper meaning regarding my chances in life. Who knows, who knows what the future would hold?

I had so much more in my pocket than the $100 that afternoon when I got off the bus in Baltimore. I had the thought I was special. I had met folks at the top of our political spectrum. I had a belief that money would just show up. I had ego or was it confidence? I could meet and talk to anyone, no matter how famous they were. No one was more than I was. But I also had seen the dogs attack kids and folks in Birmingham and knew they were braver than I was. I knew that no one deserved less than what I had and what I was. I knew that if I got sick or my tooth hurt I could go home and get it fixed, I knew I would be able to vote and could walk in to any establishment, no matter how fancy or rarified and fit in. I knew my mother in her position with Senator Sparkman would have my papers researched by the Library of Congress. I knew that when I hitch hiked, I could call home for a bus ticket.

There were weeks of hunger and little money to buy food. Weeks of living on bologna and Little Debbie Cakes. I used to run a tab at the Mount Royal Tavern till my next paycheck. But there was always a back-up, a home, with a full refrigerator and a drink, a TV and air-conditioning. My poverty was self-imposed and a journey to find all that was beyond the middle class, commercial world that I was drowning in. Many like me left for Jack's life on the road and it was a good and moral journey for us. I had chances to hang out at the Factory with Warhol, but that scene was the opposite of what I searched for and am still ok with not going down there. Meeting Jimmy Reed, the great blues player from Chicago and drinking beer with him and watching him play was better.

For me, the best thing was the failure of my parents to raise me and to secure my future with church talk and well invested money. Perhaps then I would have not of had the courage to take the risk, I was slated to be a Capitol Hill bum, that's what they called the kids with patronage jobs, secured by their political connections. I had one, could have kept it. But I did not stay in that vacuum. If they had succeeded in making me more like them I would not have become an artist/educator and not moved in the direction of empathy. Who knows, the other road could have led to a Lexus. A Lexus swerving through slow traffic with rage and terrified children. A man who could not love his family. A life spiraling to the bottom of a bottle of whiskey. A life of privilege wasted. No, thanks.

Hugh Merrill is an artist/educator, writer and community arts activist. In 1985 he had a one-person exhibition at the Nelson Atkins Museum, and his work is in the collections of over 50 major museums such as the Museum of Modern Art New York, Kemper Museum KC, Cranbrook Museum and the National Museum of Poland. In 1996 he collaborated with French artist Christian Boltanski on the city-wide community arts project *Our City Ourselves* for the Kemper Museum. He was the past president of the Southern Graphics Council International and is a long time professor at the Kansas City Art Institute. He developed Chameleon Arts and Youth Development into a resource for disenfranchised youth communities providing over 1 million dollars in community arts and youth development programming in the past 20 years. Merrill was selected as one of 42 international artists for Richard Noyce's book *Printmaking At the Edge* published in 2006. He has been awarded grants including an NEA grant, Melon Foundation, a Yaddo Fellowship, and the Distinguished Education Award from the Southern Graphics Council International 2007. In 2008 he was invited by the Nelson Atkins Museum to curate *Print Lovers at Thirty*. In September of 2009 his retrospective *Divergent Consistencies*, was exhibited by the Leedy-Voulkos Art Center. He has written *Divergent Consistencies: 40 years of studio and community artwork*, *Shared Visions: Thoughts and Experiences in Social Arts Practice 2014*, and *Preaching to the Choir: thoughts on contemporary printmaking*. Merrill also has two books of poetry, *Dog Alley* and *Nomadic*.

CPSIA information can be obtained
at www.ICGtesting.com
Printed in the USA
LVHW112342231219
641457LV00001B/153/P